JACK
NO NAME

T0346372

MELAINA
FARANDA

Published by Pearson Education Limited, Edinburgh Gate, Harlow, Essex, CM20 2JE
Registered company number: 872828

www.pearsonschools.co.uk

First published by Pearson
a division of Pearson New Zealand Ltd
67 Apollo Drive, Rosedale, North Shore 0632, New Zealand
Associated companies throughout the world

Text © Pearson 2009

Page Layout and Design: Sarah Healey

The right of Melaina Faranda to be identified as author of this work has been
asserted by her in accordance with the Copyright, Designs and Patents Act 1988.

First published 2009
This edition published 2012

2023
12

British Library Cataloguing in Publication Data
A catalogue record for this book is available from the British Library

ISBN 978-0-43507-615-3

Printed and bound in Great Britain by Ashford Colour Press Ltd.

Acknowledgements
We would like to thank the children and teachers of Bangor Central Integrated
Primary School, NI; Bishop Henderson C of E Primary School, Somerset; Brookside
Community Primary School, Somerset; Cheddington Combined School,
Buckinghamshire; Cofton Primary School, Birmingham; Dair House Independent
School, Buckinghamshire; Deal Parochial School, Kent; Lawthorn Primary School,
North Ayrshire; Newbold Riverside Primary School, Rugby and Windmill Primary
School, Oxford for their invaluable help in the development and trialling of the Bug
Club resources.

Every effort has been made to contact copyright holders of material reproduced in
this book. Any omissions will be rectified in subsequent printings if notice is given
to the publishers.

A division of Pearson New Zealand Ltd

CONTENTS

CHAPTER 1

"Take that! And that!"

Leaping high into the air, Jack thrust his weapon at the enemy. "Never more will you plague Glastonbury, evil sir."

"Jack No Name!"

Jack twisted mid-leap and stepped back ... into a steaming green cowpat. The leaves of his enemy, an ailing apple tree, seemed to shake with laughter.

Disgusting. He pulled his bare foot out and wiped it vigorously on the grass.

A monk wearing a cowled tunic of undyed wool stood by one of the apple trees, his arms folded over a long strip of dark wool cinched in by a rope girdle.

"Brother Peter?" Jack took the iron kettle helmet off his head and held the skewer sword by his side, feeling sheepish. He had thought he was well hidden in the abbey orchard, safely away from the kitchener and free to practise being a knight.

A deep phlegm-filled coughing followed but, when he finally spoke, Brother Peter did not mince words. "Go and scrub the pots or Kitchener Payne will flog you."

"Yes, sir," mumbled Jack to the departing monk's shaved head and narrow, hunched shoulders.

Brother Peter wouldn't have dared speak to a real knight like that, Jack thought furiously, as he kicked a dried cowpat from his path. Knights were rich and dignified. They were courteous and swore to be of service to women and children and the weak.

A wry inner voice suggested that knightly service probably didn't include cleaning pots.

Jack turned to skulk back through the orchard to the kitchen house with the borrowed kettle and skewer. But first he stopped to wash his soiled foot in the freezing waters of the spring that came from the conical tor brooding above the abbey. If only his real parents would come to claim him.

As he made his way through the kitchen garden, Jack was consumed by rebellious thoughts. He had been at Glastonbury Abbey for fifteen years, serving in the vast kitchen under Kitchener Payne for most of them. It wasn't even as if he was able to move up the abbey career ranks by becoming an oblate, then a novice. There was no money for that.

The kitchener, Brother Payne, who was head cook, had told Jack that the monks had found him outside the abbey gates near the almonry, where the poor came to beg for alms. He had been a naked squalling brat, mired in his own filth and blue with cold, and so they had called him Jack No Name . . .

But Brother Payne *would* say that. For all Jack knew, he could have arrived in a carved gilt cradle with a gold seal and signet ring, and the greedy monk had swallowed them whole.

Jack imagined that he was given to Glastonbury Abbey for safekeeping by noble parents and that it was too dangerous for anybody to know his true name. One day, when he could muster the courage, he would ask saintly Abbot Cedric for the truth.

A sudden grey-white blur of movement in the grass roused Jack from his brooding. A rabbit. Immediately, Jack's thoughts turned to cooking. His mouth watered at the prospect of baked rabbit with a pudding in its belly.

He would take the rabbit and skin it, leaving on its ears, then make a stuffing of grated bread and suet with finely chopped thyme, parsley, spinach, grated beets and sweet marjoram. That would be seasoned with cloves and sugar, a little cream and salt and minced dates, but he would be sparing with the cloves. Too much was overpowering; not enough lacked a certain . . . something. He would bind the mix with eggs and then stuff the rabbit, sewing it up with linen thread. The stuffed rabbit would do well with a mutton broth combined with a sauce of butter, verjuice, salt and sugar . . .

"Where have you been?"

Startled from his dreams of the perfect rabbit dish, Jack turned to see that Brother Payne had waddled all the way from his stool by the great fire to the kitchen door. Beyond him, the kitchen was a hive of activity as boys and men carted pots and turned spits, chopped vegetables and slapped the life from freshly caught fish.

The kitchener leaned heavily against the sturdy oak door frame. His hairless pink face was ruddy with exertion and his massive body, clad in a coarse brown robe, shuddered like beef jelly with each wheezy breath.

"I was picking apples for the pork sauce." Jack lied effortlessly, with the ease of long practice.

Lying must surely be against the knight's code of chivalry.

Brother Payne's pig eyes squinted as he took in

the kettle and skewer. Even from across the walled garden, Jack could smell the wine on the kitchener's breath. "Odd things to use for picking apples."

Fearful that the kitchener would flog him, Jack bent his head and shuffled his feet and tried to give the impression of being a dolt, an insect, completely unworthy of notice.

Brother Payne relaxed. Jack was no longer a threat. And their shared secret was still exactly that. Years ago, as Jack was blossoming into a talented and daring cook, Brother Payne had given himself up to the pleasures of the cellar, stocked with wines from brother abbeys in France and Spain. Under the guise of the head chef's orders, it was Jack who supervised the storage of cheeses from Cheddar, the delivery of mutton from the abbey's flocks of sheep and the harvested wheat from surrounding fields, as well as the picking of vegetables from the walled garden.

And it was Jack who decided what was to be cooked for the abbey's monks and, with a team of dedicated monks and lay brothers, cooked it. Whether it was veal or lamb pie, stewed ducks or sparrows, baked goose or pig, Brother Payne enjoyed the abbot's compliments and Jack the opportunity to sneak out occasionally and practise being a knight, using cooking pots for armour.

A stable boy at the George Inn had shown him how the squires practised for knighthood by honing their skills in games. A cast-iron cauldron could be used for putting the stone, and the iron spit poles that supported the roasting meat worked well as a javelin or fighting stick. As for the carving of meat – which the stable boy had assured him was an essential part of becoming a knight – he had been carving meat since he was old enough to hold a knife.

"Abbot Cedric has sent a message," Brother Payne grunted. "The Bishop of Bath and Wells is returned from pilgrimage in the Holy Lands and the abbot will journey to the cathedral to greet him."

Jack nodded, careful to keep his jaw slack and eyes blank. Privately, he wondered why he was being told. Too many years spent as a servant to this drunken slug made him suspicious.

"He has ordered that I will accompany him. He wishes to demonstrate to the bishop that Glastonbury Abbey possesses the finest cook in England."

Was it possible this shiny-faced pig actually believed he was even still a cook, let alone the finest in England?

"Of course you will come with me," the kitchener added. "I will need someone to scrub the pots."

Jack bowed his head so that the deceitful old monk would not see a spark of indignation. He disliked the fact that the kitchener seemed to believe his own lie, but he was equally thrilled by the chance to accompany the abbot to the Cathedral of Wells.

In all his time growing up at the abbey, Jack had never ventured further than Glastonbury's flat, endless fields. Yet Wells Cathedral was only a day's ride away. It was said to be a marvel, the most beautiful and majestic cathedral in all of England!

"When do we go?" Jack tried to make his voice humble and uninterested. For all his drunkenness, Brother Payne was cunning. If he caught any hint of excitement, he would make Jack's life even more miserable.

"Tomorrow at cock crow." The brother scratched one of several fat, rolling chins, as pale and pitted as plucked poultry. "I have been thinking about a special delicacy to serve with dinner tonight."

Jack groaned inwardly, waiting for a list of impossible ingredients. Sure enough, as Brother Payne reeled off a list of what he would need, Jack caught a mention of field mushrooms.

"Brother Payne, sir, it has not rained for three weeks. There will be no mushrooms to pick."

The monk's many chins wobbled and his pig eyes narrowed dangerously. With surprising swiftness, he picked up the fallen skewer and pointed it at Jack's throat. "If I ask for field mushrooms," he hissed, "you will find them!"

Jack stomped out of the abbey and into the main street of Glastonbury village, muttering curses beneath his breath. It was ridiculous. Somehow, he had to find field mushrooms, or conjure them up out of nothing.

The village was a higgledy-piggledy collection of crucks – cottages made from woven wattle frames plastered over with a daub of mixed mud, ox hair, straw and dung. The roofs were thatched with dried reeds. Ducks and roosters wandered the street and women sat on crude stools in their doorways spinning wool, or worked their vegetable gardens bent double.

"Good afternoon to you, Jack No Name." A heavy-set peasant woman with sweaty yellow hair plastered to her brow nodded at him as she lifted an enormous wicker basket of cabbages.

Jack roused himself from ill humour. *The knight's code: to honour and serve women, children and the weak.*

"Let me assist you, Mistress Mary." He got hold of the worn basket and helped her to lift it onto a wooden bench.

Mary Grocer plumped down on her stool with a hefty sigh, her filthy woollen tunic riding up to expose mud-crusted feet in crude leather shoes. "You're a good lad, Jack." For a moment, her pale, slightly protruding eyes searched his features, as if looking for someone. Then, with another sigh, her expression resumed its habitual blankness.

"Take a cabbage for your kindness. Not the top. They're full of the moth worm. I'll sell those to the George Inn," she said with a chuckle. "Let the pilgrims have meat with their cabbage soup, eh?"

Guiltily, Jack laughed with her and glanced over at the grand timber tavern built to accommodate pilgrims to Glastonbury.

Outside the George Inn, a stable boy was saddling a horse beside a small knot of pilgrims, made distinct by their brightly dyed clothing – reds and greens and yellows – and the fact that, unlike everyone else in the village, they were not occupied with a task. Their outsized crucifixes and crude souvenirs – poorly carved figurines of King Arthur and Queen Guinevere, supposedly buried in a hollowed oak trunk in the abbey grounds – shouted that they were tourists.

Like most of the other villagers, Jack regarded the pilgrims with a mix of contempt and envy. They might be clueless and easy prey for a maker of shoddy toys or a painted copper ring said to have been Guinevere's, but they brought business and precious coins to Glastonbury, as well as stories and news from the wider world.

And recipes.

Every visitor to Glastonbury Abbey who wandered by the kitchen was accosted by Jack for news of the latest food creations being served in larger towns and grander courts. These recollections he memorised, dish by dish.

There was no other way. Even if vellum and parchment had not been so impossibly expensive and hard to come by, Jack had only been taught the basics of lettering. Sometimes he suspected that Brother Payne had been ordered to teach him more, for Abbot Cedric was justly proud of the abbey as a centre of learning. But the kitchener was lazy and no doubt didn't want his pupil knowing more than he did. Still, Jack dreamed of one day creating a book of cookery – a book illuminated with swirling letters and skilful flourishes that made grown men weep at its beauty.

It was all very fine learning new dishes, but the pilgrims Jack liked best would never stoop to speak to him – beautiful ladies who were carried in palanquins or rode in intricately carved carriages. When the curtains were drawn back, it was possible to glimpse the fine-spun wool of their gowns and the gossamer veils covering their high-browed white faces, which never saw the sun.

Jack sometimes wondered if his mother was one of these women. He dreamed that she came occasionally, disguised as a pilgrim, to visit the abbey and lay a red rose upon Guinevere's grave, all the while searching the grounds through her veil, looking for her only son . . .

"Dreaming like that will land you in trouble, Jack," Mary Grocer said sharply, waking him from his daydream.

Jack shook himself and turned away from the woman's pale, penetrating gaze. Had she known what he was thinking? There were stories of people who could read other's minds.

But these were only stories, like those fed to the pilgrim tourists. They told of a fairy world beneath the tor; of darker green rings of grass that were trod by fairies; and of the corn dollies, which stood guard on either side of a thatched roof's eaves, coming to life.

Jack straightened and threw back his shoulders, refusing to believe that Mary Grocer possessed any special talent other than that of growing fat cabbages. Abbot Cedric himself had rejected the possibility of any mortal having the power to read another's mind.

"The devil got your tongue, Jack?" Mary's look was sly.

Jack shook his head and continued on his way.

"What about your cabbage?" she called after him. Her eyes were softer now, as if she were sorry she had teased him. "You could take it for church tithing!" she added hopefully.

Jack shook his head once more. Every peasant must give one-tenth of all they produced to the abbey as a tithe. He knew that a tenth of Mary Grocer's rows of cabbages, wormy or not, was far greater than a single cabbage.

"Give it to the pilgrims," Jack replied, not looking back. "It is field mushrooms I need and, before you say more, mistress, I know I won't be finding them in a month of Sundays."

Behind him, the peasant woman snorted. "No such thing as a month of Sundays when Sunday has no meaning, for it is work as usual for everyone but a monk. But, if it's mushrooms you want, Jack No Name, there are some about."

Jack turned eagerly. "Where?"

Mary's pale eyes gleamed as she threw him a cabbage, one taken from deep inside the basket. "On top of the tor."

Jack's heart sank like a bone in clear soup.

CHAPTER 2

Jack trudged miserably up the sloping street through the usual throng of filthy children chasing scrawny chickens and mangy dogs that scavenged from the open sewer running along the roadside. He passed the familiar sight of a newly butchered pig – a sticky red mess buzzing with flies – without so much as a second glance. His ears were also deaf to the smithy's clanging of hammer against molten metal. He dreaded climbing the tor.

"Watch it!"

Jack was nearly swiped by a thatcher staggering beneath a huge bundle of reeds cut by the stream, and a scattering of stalks dropped from his load. He was lucky it was reeds and not straw from the abbey barn, for it was ruled that a peasant might take as much straw as he could carry from the abbey farmyard but, if the band broke before he passed through the yard, he would lose his straw and be fined.

Further up, a far grander building than the peasants' crucks was in progress – the stone walls, door and window lintels were already in place. The roof's wood rafters were exposed, like bones awaiting a skin of thatch. This, Jack decided, was most likely intended as a new home for a merchant.

At last he had reached the calm of Chalice Well. Pilgrims ventured here to say their prayers and fill their pigs' bladders and flasks with the red-tinged water. It was claimed that it had the miraculous power of healing. This was the water Abbot Cedric used for communion in the Lady Chapel.

Jack put down the cabbage and splashed his hands and face. The water was icy and had a slightly metallic taste, as though he had been hiding a copper coin in his cheek to keep it safe from the kitchener.

From the well, a hill rose sharply through a wood of oaks, hawthorns, yews and beeches to the tor. It was said that once, long ago, an abbey monk had ventured on to the tor and returned days later gibbering with fear. He had never recovered his wits or the power of speech. Abbot Cedric had long since forbidden any of the brothers from climbing the conical slope of the tor.

A few years before, Jack had not understood this edict. Or perhaps he had understood and decided to disobey anyway, consumed by curiosity. As he climbed, the tor had seemed at first like an ordinary hill, if oddly shaped: a tall, conical mountain with a wide path spiralling around it like a maze. From the top, however, Jack had been able to see down over the meadows in their final stage of ploughing, stretching out to the salt marshes to the south. In the west, he had even glimpsed a silver glint of sea.

More remarkable than the land rolling like waves in every direction was the sensation that had raced through him – a surge that bubbled up through his bare feet and burned behind his forehead like a brand. Down below, the abbey that contained all of his life had seemed trifling, a tiny place compared to the world that stretched out in every direction. He was filled with power. Suddenly, Jack had been certain that he could be what he'd always wished to be – a knight!

A shepherd had seen him on the tor and had snitched to the prior. Jack's punishment had been at the hands of Kitchener Payne and it had been severe. After that, Jack could never pass the wet rope kept coiled in a wooden pail without shuddering.

Now, it was not so much the memory of the

kitchener's cruelty that dragged at Jack's feet as he climbed. He was afraid of himself: of that wild spark of freedom; of that strange and wonderful feeling of power racing through his body . . .

Jack trudged up the spiralling path, holding his worm-free cabbage and scanning the cow-mown grass for the silvery discs of field mushrooms. Near the top, he resisted a strange compulsion to lie down on the earth and watch the floating clouds and determinedly kept up his search.

At the summit, Jack took a deep breath and forgot the mushrooms. Below, the meadows stretched in a shimmering gold haze as far as he could see. In the town, tiny toy people bustled along the streets. Rising up from the village's midst was the familiar honeyed stone of the abbey, with its noble arches. The lead tiles of the kitchen roof were visible, surrounded by a square of garden. Beyond it, sheep grazed in the apple orchard.

Here was his whole world, laid out like an illuminated manuscript. Tomorrow, Jack knew he would move beyond it – into another realm. He would visit the miraculous Cathedral of Wells.

A faint tinkle of bells caused Jack to spin around.

An old woman stood within arm's reach, gazing

at him gravely. Her face was etched with wrinkles and she wore a strange assortment of clothes – layered, faded rags in what must once have been brilliant scarlets, golds and blues. Over her shoulder was a grimy bag fashioned from another square of worn cloth.

How did she get here? Jack was certain he had been the only one climbing the tor.

He inched away. He had heard the stories about the fairies that lived in the tor. Everyone had. But fairies were supposed to be beautiful maids in shimmering dresses. He couldn't remember a single story where a fairy assumed the form of an old lady with two blackcurrant eyes that had been dropped in skimmed curd.

Looking more closely, Jack saw that the old woman's mouth was pursed and white-edged, as if she were in pain. His guess was confirmed when she moved, raising a faint tinkle of bells that seemed to come from her ankles, and winced.

Service to women and children and the weak and the poor.

"Are you all right, mistress?"

"I have injured my knee," she said slowly. "I fell upon a rock."

Although she spoke the King's English, her

accent was sharp and strange, unlike the broad, homey speech and soft burr of the Glastonbury village folk.

Jack resisted the impulse to ask why she had climbed the tor with an injury. Instead he asked, "Can I help you back to your home?"

She shook her head, her eyes vacant. "I have no home."

Jack's mind raced. Although Abbot Cedric had ordained that the poor and needy should always be cared for, it was hit and miss when it came to who served as almoner upon the gate. If the old woman begged alms from Brother Peter, for instance, she would be lucky to go from the gates with yesterday's brown bread and some stern words about begging.

If, however, she were lucky enough to encounter Prior John, or many of the other monks, she would be given a warm meal of meat and a bed in the infirmary until she was well enough to walk without pain.

Without pain . . . Jack became aware of the ridiculous cabbage tucked beneath his arm. Cabbage could be used as a medicine. It was also particularly good with blood sausage, fennel seeds and leeks. After stripping off the large outer leaves, Jack tore off a modest-sized leaf and handed it to her.

"This will help you with the swelling."

The leaf hung limp in the old woman's hand as she continued to gaze at him, *through* him.

Jack sighed. "Sit down, mistress, and I will bind it to your knee."

The knee was livid red and swollen to three times a normal size. "This should help," murmured Jack as he bound the leaf to her knee with a strip of tattered linen.

When it was done, the sun was already slanting dark gold over the fields and dusk's shadows were gathering in pockets of woodland below.

"I must go," he said, relieved to take leave of this strange old woman. He turned to race back down the path but, before he was out of her line of sight, something seemed to pull him up short like an invisible rope, dragging him back.

I swear to serve women and children, the weak and the poor.

"Mistress, may I help you back down the tor?"

As Jack pulled the old woman to her feet, a slow smile dawned on her pain-racked face. "Young master, for your kindness I shall tell you what I see. You are going on a journey. If you succeed in your quest, a great peace will be brought to the West Country and you will learn your true name."

"My true name!"

She nodded.

Then, as Jack replayed her words in his head, something occurred to him. "You said *if* I succeed?"

A horn blared from below the tor. It was not the sound of the shepherds driving their flocks into the pen, or the cow-man herding the cows back to the byre to keep them safe from thieves and wolves.

Jack frowned and turned to look down. The horn blared again and this time he recognised the sound: a hunting horn. He shivered. Who led a hunt at the start of nightfall?

He had to get back down to the abbey and take the old lady somewhere safe. If hounds were loosed, they shouldn't be anywhere out in the open.

Turning back, Jack gasped. The old woman had vanished. There was only the outline of where her frail body had rested on the dewy grass. Next to it sat her grimy bundle.

Jack picked it up. It felt surprisingly light and soft. Peeling back a fold of cloth, he saw silvery discs gleaming in the dying light. Field mushrooms.

Jack threw himself into a dense hedge as a dark horse

clattered past at breakneck speed, its hooves ringing against the hard-baked earth of the track leading up to the base of the tor. The rider swung the horse about sharply. It reared, then smashed down to the ground again.

Cowering against the hedge, Jack prayed that the rider had not turned for him. The tunnel of trees blocked the dying light and created an eerie purple-black twilight. A stray bit of hedge tickled his nose, smelling green and slightly citric. An infusion of these leaves might work well in a capon sauce ...

"Boy!"

The rider's voice was harsh above the snorting and pawing of his steed. His robes were black and, judging by their sheen, very fine. A dark hood obscured his face. From the cut of his cloth and the sleekness of his horse, it was obvious that he was wealthy. A pilgrim strayed too far at night? Then why did he have a silver hunting horn slung over one shoulder?

Jack pressed closer to the hedge, wishing he could be back among the warm smells of the abbey kitchen. Something squishy was cushioning him from the worst of the prickly hedge. The mushrooms. Kitchener Payne was going to kill him.

"I am looking for someone," continued the rider.

And whoever it was probably wasn't going to be happy when he found them.

Conceding defeat, Jack untangled himself from the hedge and shrugged, only just remembering to let his face slacken into servile stupidity. "I . . . I have to get back to my master," he mumbled.

The man spoke scornfully. "If you can help me there will be a silver coin for your reward."

Now that was more like it. And not just a copper coin, either – a silver coin. Jack thought happily about all the souvenirs in Wells he'd be able to buy with that. Maybe a carved copy of the moon clock? There might even be enough to buy a pink ribbon for the woodcutter's daughter . . .

"Yes, sir," said Jack, standing to attention – just like a squire to a knight! "I will help you as best as I can."

"It's an old crone I'm looking for. Ugly, withered . . . I believe she may have met with a nasty fall. Best to relieve her of her misery."

Jack's heart sank. The old woman on the tor – and, from the sound of it, the man did not wish her well.

I swear to honour and protect women, children, the weak and the poor.

"I haven't seen any such old woman, sir." He was

good at lying, but he had delayed too long.

With whip-like speed, the rider's hand snaked down and seized Jack by the coarsely woven scruff of his tunic. "Listen here, boy," he hissed from beneath the black hood. "I don't like liars and I don't like being made a fool of. Where I come from, we have a punishment for liars."

With his other hand, he loosed the bridle and drew a shining dagger from beneath his velvet tunic.

Jack gulped. "It's true," he said, "that I thought I saw, not where I just came from, but before . . . Before, I think I saw a strange old woman setting off across . . . the fields near Chalice Well." Jack cursed himself. It was a poor lie, poorly performed.

"She cannot get far. The scourge will reach her, as it will them all," the man muttered. "In which direction did she go?"

Dry-mouthed, Jack lied again. "To the west, sir."

Immediately, the man loosened his grip and sheathed his dagger.

"What about my coin?" Jack asked, keen now to play the part of a cowardly village boy who would sell an old woman's soul for an apple seed.

The man's silence made Jack shudder, even as a glint of metal arced through the air. In the cloud of dust kicked up by the departing horse, Jack scrabbled in the earth for the coin. It was copper.

And the horseman did not go in the direction Jack had indicated. Instead, he continued on to the tor.

CHAPTER 3

Kitchener Payne would not only kill him, he would skewer and roast him over the fire. And, no doubt, burn him to charcoal. A small part of Jack was pleased that the fat old monk would finally have to get off his suet behind and cook. The larger part, however, knew that Brother Payne would drunkenly add the wrong herbs or over-spice the dishes. And then, when the complaints came back from the abbey dining room, he would blame it on that stupid kitchen boy. He quickened his pace in the direction of the abbey.

"Boy!"

Not again, thought Jack irritably. Who was it this time?

A girl stepped from the shadows. Even in the near-darkness, Jack could see that, beneath the grime and ragged clothing, she was quite possibly pretty. Could *she* be a fairy in disguise?

"Have you seen an old woman near about?"

Jack examined her more closely before he replied – a girl with matted red hair and a glimmer of tears in her eyes. She seemed distinctly less dangerous than the dark-robed rider. He nodded. "Up on the tor."

"And the rider?"

"I told him she had gone west through Chalice Well fields."

The girl looked momentarily relieved until the triumphant sound of a horn high up on the tor shattered the evening stillness. She turned to him, stricken.

"He didn't believe me," added Jack, flinching at the expression on her face. To his horror, the girl fell to her knees and beat her hands against the earth, sobbing with low animal moans that reminded Jack of the abbey's cattle when their calves had been taken for veal.

"He has taken her!" she cried. "He has taken her!"

"Please get up," Jack urged. He moved to help her rise, then hesitated. Was touching a pretty young girl in distress, even a grubby one with tangled locks, permissible by the knight's code of conduct?

Stuff the knight's code with rosemary, rue and a pinch of thyme.

Jack raised her up and felt his heart beat harder as she leaned her face into his chest and sobbed.

"I must help her," she said, finally pulling away.

"Help her?" Jack echoed uselessly.

"The scourge – it has begun."

"What is the scourge?" Jack asked, then wished he hadn't. He remembered now – he had heard mention of it from Jonas. The scourge was a hunt for witches. So the old woman was . . . not a fairy but a witch? Is that why she had been able to vanish so suddenly? But, if she could vanish, then why not from the man who hunted her? "Your grandmother is . . . a witch?" Jack breathed.

The girl sniffed and rubbed her wet eyes with fury. "Not a witch!" she snapped. "Those they call witches are only wise women who have the gifts of healing."

"But why have they begun a scourge! Why now?" Jack asked.

The girl fixed him with large, red-rimmed eyes. "The Bishop of Bath and Wells is dead. Robert Fox has menaced the priests into accepting him as bishop in his stead. And Robert Fox has a great fear and horror of witches."

"The bishop is dead? But that can't be!" Jack exclaimed. "I am going with Abbot Cedric to visit the bishop tomorrow."

Disbelief showed clearly in the girl's downturned mouth.

"It's true," Jack insisted.

Her delicate eyebrows arched.

"All right then," he confessed. "I am going, but as the cook's boy."

This time, a glimmer of amusement appeared in the girl's sad, tawny eyes. "The bishop died a week ago of the plague. I am surprised your abbot does not yet know. Although . . ."

"What?" Jack demanded.

"Grandmother predicted the bishop's fate long ago. It's why we fled to Glastonbury – to bring warning, for Robert Fox will hunt every woman he thinks to be a witch, every midwife and healer across the land."

"Glastonbury?"

"Here is where he will hunt the hardest. He and his pack of clerical hounds." The girl's voice rang out clear and bell-like through the tree-shadowed twilight.

Jack shivered. He felt a great urgency to escape this strange, demanding girl and return to the safety of the abbey. "I have to go."

Hands on her hips, she stared at him. Fury made

her even prettier. "You're going to leave me here alone, just like that?"

"Er . . . yes. You see, I have to be back at the abbey or Brother Payne will –"

"A knight's code of conduct is to honour and protect women, children and the poor and weak," the girl declared. "I qualify for at least two of those. Abbot Cedric would want you to provide me with shelter and food. He is a kind man and, I believe," she added, "he will be greatly interested to learn of the Bishop of Bath and Well's death before a messenger arrives. It is vital that he learn what is afoot."

It was probably true, Jack reflected reluctantly. He should help her. She was fortunate that the abbot had chosen to live in the abbey these past months, rather than in any of the fine manor houses available to him.

It was more than that, though. Something was tugging at the back of his mind. He felt somehow responsible. His failure to lie convincingly had led the rider directly to her grandmother. "I will take you as far as the abbey gates," he said. "Then we will have to part or I'll be in even *more* trouble."

The girl slipped into an easy pace beside him. "My name is Lara," she said conversationally, "and you and I will not be parted for long." She tugged at his bundle of now thoroughly battered mushrooms. They gave off a pungent fungal smell.

"Grandmother gave you a gift. Now you have an obligation to her, and to me to help find her."

Jack muttered under his breath. Those cursed field mushrooms. He should have known there was no such thing as a free lunch – or dinner . . .

"You stay here," Jack said. "Evening prayers will be finished. I'll see if I can rouse the abbot."

Lara nodded, clearly impatient. They had come to the farm gate entrance to the abbey. Although it was dark, Jack wanted to be sure to avoid inquisitive looks and prying questions from those not already preparing for bed in the dormitory.

Jack pushed against the thick bars of the iron gate and was pleased to feel it creak open. Jonas, the oblate whose task it was to guard the back gate, was nowhere in sight. He had been entered into the monastery against his will and was forever sneaking away to visit the pot maid from the George Inn.

Jack crept through the abbey grounds, careful not to set the dogs barking. In the cool night air he could pick out the scent of mint and sweet marjoram. An owl hooted from the orchard and crickets chorused like chanting monks.

The abbot's palace was built grand and high in the same honeyed stone as the rest of the abbey. Beneath the window slit of Abbot Cedric's bed chamber, Jack peered up at the orange bar of light cast by candles rolled from the wax of the abbey's own hives. The abbot was back from prayer. Unlike the other monks, who must bed down together on straw pallets in the dormitory, the abbot needed time for private thought and prayer.

All very well, Jack thought, but how would he, a mere kitchen servant, be able to convince the procession of high-ranking monks who must be got through before he could see the abbot?

Creeping to the grand wooden door, Jack tugged at a hemp rope dangling from a bronze bell, then darted behind the cover of a small, thorny tree.

The door cracked open and a hooded face peered out. It was impossible to tell whose. And now a telltale cough split the night – deep and phlegm-filled. Brother Peter!

"Who's there?" the monk called. He stepped towards the thorn tree, coming closer to the lad cowering behind it, and spat onto the grass. Then he spun around and returned inside. The door thudded shut behind him.

Scooping up a small stone, Jack threw it furiously against the wall. It ricocheted off and stung his shoulder. He was tempted to pretend that the girl and her grandmother really had been strange fairy visions so that he could go back to the kitchen. But the girl's sorrowful amber eyes and her grandmother's swollen knee had been real enough . . .

With a sigh, Jack picked up another pebble. This time, it arced up and entered the window slit. The tapestry that usually hung over it had been pinned back to allow the bracing night air to keep the abbot wakeful at his prayers.

The abbot's face appeared in the crack of window, his bare, shaved head silvery in the starlight. Jack froze.

"Who's there?" Abbot Cedric called.

"It . . . It's . . . me," Jack stammered. "Jack No Name – the kitchen boy."

"Jack No Name . . ." The abbot sounded astonished. In the abbey hierarchy, Jack was an ant, even ranked below the runaway oblate, Jonas. "Want to apologise for ruining that lamb stew?" asked Abbot Cedric after a long pause. "Inedible. I had to order my monks to fast until the morning."

Furious, Jack pictured Kitchener Payne's shifty

eyes darting from side to side in his lying pig face.

"But I was up on . . ." He stopped himself in time. He had been up on the *tor*. A place the abbot had forbidden the monks to visit. Helping an old lady, possibly a . . . *witch*. His mind buzzed with rage at Brother Payne, but through it another thought occurred. If the abbot had complained about the meal, then the kitchener could well be wetting the hemp rope to punish him for it.

"Abbot Cedric, sir," Jack said. "I wish to speak with you about another matter."

"Well, Jack No Name, speak plainly. I must finish my prayers."

Jack looked around. An owl hooted and a cow lowed restively. "Sir, it is not something I wish the world to hear."

Abbot Cedric laughed – a sweet laugh that fitted his saintly, if sometimes stern, reputation. "What could you say that would not be fit for the ears of all of God's creatures?"

"No," said Jack, desperate now. "It is an urgent matter intended for your ears alone, for there is great danger in it. There is someone outside the gates who has an important message for you."

The room darkened, as if a violent breeze had guttered the candle, and the shaved head vanished.

"Abbot?" Jack called.

There was no reply.

Despondent, Jack turned to creep back to the gates. Not only had he failed to secure an audience for Lara, he would also, no doubt, be forced to do penance for it. Though what could be greater penance than a drunken Brother Payne and a wet rope?

At the sound of the grand entrance door sighing open, Jack turned to see Abbot Cedric step out, carrying a flaming torch that lit up his wizened features. He took hold of Jack's arm to steady himself on the uneven ground.

Jack led the abbot to the back gate, amazed. He hoped he did not smell too badly of cabbage and dirt. Here he was, the kitchen boy, arm-in-arm with a man who was practically a saint – the Abbot of Glastonbury!

Jack fidgeted with the kitchen brazier, poking in the last roundels of apple-wood to make the fire sweet-scented and brighter burning.

Beside him, the abbot and Lara were deep in discussion, their heads bent towards one another. The abbot's hood was pulled back from a shaved scalp like a silvery crescent moon; the girl's red head resembled a tangle of flames.

"You say the Bishop of Bath and Wells is dead of plague!" the abbot exclaimed.

Lara nodded, then lifted a spoonful of watery lamb stew to her lips and slurped down the liquid. "Ugh. This is terrible!"

The abbot looked at Jack, yet the girl continued to eat greedily, with only the occasional grimace.

"We were to visit him tomorrow," Abbot Cedric said. "He has only just returned from the Crusade. When did this happen?"

"Seven days ago."

Jack was fascinated by the girl's lack of awe in the presence of this holy man. He was used to the villagers trembling with excitement if the old man so much as deigned to glance at them during a special service. This girl, however – surely no older than himself – treated the abbot as an equal.

"What is your name, child?" the abbot enquired.

"Lara."

"And you came direct from Wells?" Disbelief stretched the abbot's gaunt features so that, for a moment, Jack could almost see the skull beneath blue-white skin that never felt the kiss of the sun.

"As directly as we might with Robert Fox's men

swarming," the girl agreed.

"Why has no messenger been sent to me from the cathedral?"

"I am your messenger," said Lara bluntly. "There will not be one from the cathedral for as long as Robert Fox can prevent it. The bishop's will has not been found and the King will not visit for fear of the plague. In the absence of a will, he has agreed with the priests to appoint Robert Fox as regent for the bishopric.

At this mention of Robert Fox, Jack was intrigued to see the abbot's face blanch even whiter.

"You say Robert Fox is crowned bishop?" Abbot Cedric asked.

"Acting bishop," Lara corrected, "but with all the bishop's powers. If I were you, sir, I would journey even more swiftly to Wells. Robert Fox must be challenged."

The abbot nodded in slow agreement. A look came into his eyes – a look that transformed him from a sweet old man into a leader blazing with power.

So this was how he had managed to rise through the ranks of backbiters to become abbot.

"Why do you tell me this, Lara?" the abbot asked. "What is it that you want?"

Lara put down the pot of ruined lamb stew and fixed the abbot with amber eyes that were equally radiant with power. "I want safe passage with you to Wells."

Abbot Cedric nodded, cautious. "And that is all?"

She shook her tangled red locks so that they kindled once more in the light of the crackling fire. "Robert Fox's hell hounds have captured my grandmother."

"Your grandmother?"

Lara's eyes widened, as if staring at some far-off, terrible vision. "A scourge has begun."

CHAPTER 4

"Your hair," moaned Jack, protesting in spite of himself.

Lara's hair had been cut to her ears, though, mercifully, the abbot had stopped short of a full shave.

Lara pushed Jack squarely in the chest, like the boy she was pretending to be. "Hair will grow again, but brains can't. Poor you."

Jack checked a powerful impulse to shove her back. *Knights never harmed women or children or the poor and the weak.*

He had been feeling sorry for her, what with her grandmother and the scourge. Perhaps it was the bright morning sunshine, lending a glossy shine to the apple trees surrounding them, or the larks soaring overhead – but she seemed altogether too cheerful.

"What about the scourge?" he asked acidly. "Heads don't grow back, either." As soon as the words were out of his mouth, he wished he could cram them back in with a fistful of pepper and raw garlic as penance.

Lara's amber eyes clouded over, becoming brown and troubled. "Don't for a moment think that I have forgotten my grandmother, kitchen boy," she hissed. She reached up, picked an apple and bit into it with a savage crunch. "Sunlight and pure water, lark song and ripe red apples must be enjoyed while we are here," she said, before pegging the apple straight at his gut.

Jack only just caught it. When he threw it back, Lara caught it neatly, picked another two apples and began juggling the three of them high in the air.

"What's this?"

Jack turned to see Brother Payne wobbling by on his way back to the kitchen, his massive girth shaking beneath his greasy brown gown.

The monk peered at Lara as she stood holding the apples tight against the stained and patched tunic that Abbot Cedric had insisted Jack give her. Now, the clothes Jack was wearing were all that he possessed.

Brother Payne's pig eyes were red-rimmed from

a night of steady drinking. "You must be the new kitchen boy Brother Peter has told me of."

"Yes," Lara said.

"Yes, sir!" Brother Payne boomed.

"Yes, sir!" Her mimicry was superb.

Jack gazed, transfixed, as the spider veins on the monk's cheeks turned purple-black. If Lara kept this up, the kitchener would have the wet rope out in no time.

"What's your name, boy?"

"Nash, sir."

"What kind of heathen name is that?" the monk roared.

Lara remained calm. "You are a famous cook, Brother Payne. It is an honour to be travelling with you to Wells."

The kitchener squinted at her suspiciously, as if wondering if this was more disguised cheekiness. Lara kept her face carefully blank.

At last, Brother Payne grunted and turned back to the kitchen. Lara flashed Jack a grin. "Let's go."

"W-where to?" Jack asked. "We still have to pack the kitchen things into the carts."

"To the medicine garden," Lara said.

Jack stared at her blankly.

"The abbey *does* have one?"

"Of course, the infirmary garden is behind that orchard."

"Then we will pick some valerian, passion flower, chamomile and wood betony to ease the journey for our dear Brother Payne."

Jack stared, admiring and envious. Once, from spite, he had slipped pepper and prune juice into the kitchener's ale, but he had never thought of drugging the old pig before.

When Jack looked back, Glastonbury Tor was a pimple in the distance. His backside was stiff and his legs ached. Though his piebald pony trotted amiably enough along the rutted road, he couldn't help looking wistfully at the abbot's fine carriage, pulled by four white geldings.

It would take the better part of the day to reach Wells. Abbot Cedric had decided it was most urgent to travel straight through and not break the journey with a meal at a neighbouring manor, as was the usual custom.

Ten monks and seven burly lay brothers had accompanied them – men toughened by farming and heavy work. Jack wondered if these men had been included to deter any attack from robbers in the Mendip hills, or if the abbot anticipated greater danger at Wells . . .

In front of Jack, the snoring kitchener was laid out upon a cart, his nose purpling in the warm sunshine.

Lara trotted up to Jack on her pony and let go of the bridle to gesture at a blue-hazed hill in the distance. As he clung to his own reins, Jack felt envious of her skilful horsemanship.

"See that hill?" Lara asked.

He nodded.

"Wells lies beyond it."

"Do you know all of the countryside?" he asked.

Lara laughed. "Grandmother and I travel. We have many homes. All through the Mendips there are caves that are like palaces."

"I would love to see those caves," Jack confessed.

Lara's curious amber eyes regarded him. "One day," she said, without a hint of laughter, "you will."

Ahead, the abbot's carriage was drawing up under the shade of an enormous oak. As one, the accompanying monks dismounted, tying their horses to the low-slung branches of an oak trimmed to escape the ravages of passing goats.

One of the monks sat down by the kitchen cart and Jack's heart quickened. It was time for their meal. He slid from the pony and landed jarringly on a tree root.

"Brother Payne," he said, making a big show of shaking the monk awake. "We must prepare the abbot's lunch."

A tearing snore was the only response.

"He will not wake!" There were murmurings of discontent from the hungry men.

"No doubt he is wearied after loading the kitchen cart," said Abbot Cedric, his blue eyes as kind as always.

Jack bit his lip to stop from protesting. He and Lara had loaded the cart entirely by themselves.

"The kitchen boys will serve in his stead."

Jack tried not to smile. This was his chance. He would be able to demonstrate his skills to the abbot after all.

Jack pulled an oak trencher from the cart and unwrapped a woven cloth to reveal loaves of fresh-baked wheat bread that had come from the ovens before dawn. From another water-dampened cloth, he drew out a pat of the abbey's finest butter. This, Jack smeared onto thick slices of bread. To these he added goat cheese, finely sliced red apples from the orchard for a balancing sweetness, a pinch of salt, a dusting of cracked pepper and scattered fennel tips.

He was about to serve the slices of bread on trenchers when Lara came up with a handful of herbs. "Sorrel," she said. "I picked it a while back."

Jack's eyes narrowed, but he took a leaf of the sorrel, tore it and immediately recognised that its citrusy tartness would offset the sweetness of the apple to perfection.

The monks seemed to agree, for everyone ate with gusto. Abbot Cedric even declared that Jack had atoned for last night before helping himself to another piece of bread.

Afterwards, Jack served the rest of the apples and cheese smeared with woodland honey. As he packed the trenchers back into the cart, he felt a sense of contentment. It wasn't the same as rescuing maidens from towers, or jousting evil knights, but serving people a good meal made Jack feel as if he had achieved something.

Some way further on their journey, they came to a village from which blue smoke rose amid shouts of pain and confusion.

Abbot Cedric gestured for silence from his party and they all listened to the terrible, heart-rending screams. A piercing female voice was crying, "No, I beg you. Don't. Please don't!"

Then came a heavy splash.

"What is it?" blurted Jack, his skin prickling with horror at the sudden silence.

Lara's eyes shone with tears. "It is the scourge. We have to help!"

The lay brothers and monks nearest them muttered dissent. It was their work to protect the abbot and they had left the boundaries of abbey lands. It would not be politic to intervene in village affairs. That was for the village lord to determine.

But Lara rode her little russet pony over to where Abbot Cedric watched the coiling smoke through misted eyes before bending his shaved head in prayer. "Abbot Cedric!" she cried. "We must do something!"

The abbot raised his eyes to her anguished face. "We are not knights, child. We are monks and men of peace."

Jack saw how Lara's knuckles turned white upon the reins. "These villagers are innocent of any crime but incurring Robert Fox's blind hatred."

Her words seemed to rouse the abbot. "You are right," he said, and called to his monks. "We will ride in. We will do what we must to protect the weak and innocent."

The village was much smaller than Glastonbury and, Jack noted, as he rode at the tail of the abbot's party, poorer, too. There was a mill and a bakehouse, but the church was crude timber and piled stone and had no pretensions to the soaring arches of Glastonbury Abbey.

The abbot ordered his men to stop in the shadow of the mill. From there they could spy on events through a gap in the buildings.

Gathered near the millpond were twenty or so people dressed in the usual peasant garb of brown homespun woollen garments. Circling them on horseback were men in hooded black robes. An odd grey-brown shape bobbed among the rushes in the millpond.

Jack turned, sickened, as two men hooked poles into the bubbling, waterlogged fabric and dragged from the pond a drowned woman with moon-white skin and hair that must once have been as red as Lara's.

A small, filthy child struggled from a woman's arms and broke free to scramble towards the sodden corpse. "Mama!"

The collective intake of breath among the villagers

was broken only by the child's ragged sobs.

"Where my dada?" the child was asking now, as tear trails cut two silver lines down his grimy cheeks. The woman who had held the child came forward to gather him close again, shushing and whispering. "He's out with the sheep and will be back soon."

One of the men on horseback looked at the drowned body with grim distaste. "Villagers, you have accused one of your own. You told me that this woman, Agnes, gathered herbs in the moonlight. You said that this woman tended the miller when he was fevered and killed him with her herbs. You said she favoured her left hand and was seen to speak to herself often and sing songs with strange words."

The muttering villagers were cowed into silence as the man's voice thundered on. "Agnes did not float! She has been tested and was not a witch! Not long ago, I am told, part of the church's roof collapsed. One of you tells me that her sheep have got the foot rot. Last year a child was born here with six toes! There is still a witch among you, cursing your sheep and goats, causing you illness and calamity."

Terror struck the little gathering and they began to glance at each other with dread suspicion.

Now the rider's voice turned gentle and coaxing. "Think carefully. Who among you, in the guise of neighbour, friend, perhaps even wife, secretly wishes you ill? Who wished the miller ill?"

A woman shouted, "It was Jane, sir. The miller's wife. She was the only other who attended him. She must have fed him poisonous toadstools."

At this there were shouts of agreement.

"I am innocent!" cried one of the women.

Jack saw that she was more finely dressed than the others and was plump where the other village women were little more than skin and bones. Her hair was combed and her cheeks rosy. He could see, in a village as poor as this, why she might be envied.

"Why does Bertha know so much about toadstools?" countered Jane, but already a man in black had seized her. He dragged her to the edge of the millpond.

"Enough killing," Cedric Abbot muttered disgustedly. "Stay here," he ordered his men, and he hastened from their hiding place to position himself directly between the miller's widow and the pond.

CHAPTER 5

"In God's name what is taking place here?" Abbot Cedric cried.

Furious, the rider stepped his horse closer and pushed back his black hood to reveal a shaved head. "Do not interrupt God's business."

"Do not threaten me!"

From where he watched behind the corner of the mill, Jack was stunned to see the saintly abbot's white-hot blaze of indignation. "I am the Abbot of Glastonbury! I *am* a man of God. And who are you?"

At this revelation, the rider did not seem so much intimidated as elated. "Then you have come to join us in ensuring the will of God prevails and that all witches are scourged from the world?"

"On whose authority do you come here and murder the innocent?"

"I am given direct authority by Robert Fox, Bishop of Bath and Wells."

The abbot's face darkened. "Robert Fox has not been ordained bishop."

At this the rider sneered. "He is as good as. The King has declared him regent, and the bishop regent has declared a scourge – starting in the West Country. There is a reward for every witch found and destroyed."

The abbot held firm to his purpose. "I believe that the former bishop's will has yet to be found. It is one reason I travel to Wells. When the will is found, you will be rewarded with harsh penances for each and every one of these murders."

The two men glared at each other.

"You are no longer on Glastonbury lands," the rider muttered, but Jack could see that he was uncertain.

"Perhaps not, but when Robert Fox is deposed . . ."

The rider drew a sharp breath at this, as if the abbot had suggested heresy. "You are a friend of witches then, Abbot?"

Abbot Cedric's reply was grim. "I try to be a friend to all people of the Earth, as Our Lord was. What you are doing is wrongful."

"I will return to Wells," muttered the rider, "and

warn the new bishop to prepare for your arrival."

Abbot Cedric nodded, his expression cool.

As the rider gestured for his men to follow and they galloped from the village, Jack felt a dull ache creep upon him. Abbot Cedric would not be safe in Wells.

When the abbot beckoned, Jack went with Lara and the monks to join him.

"You have done great evil here today," the abbot scolded the knot of villagers, white-faced with confusion and shock. "You have accused each other of foul doings and an innocent woman is dead."

"What should we do?" a woman moaned.

"Give her a Christian burial," said Abbot Cedric, "and see that a stone is set upon her grave to serve as a reminder. Where is your priest? Who is your confessor?"

A timid-looking man slunk from the knot of villagers, wearing the same coarse, patched robes as the rest of them.

Abbot Cedric's furious frown gave way to a great weariness. It was obvious, even to Jack, that this priest was only a villager whose knowledge of farming had raised him up to count the tithes of grain and animals to be turned into church coin on market days.

The abbot sighed. "I will hear each and every one of your confessions." Reaching deep into his robe, he pulled out a leather purse and took out a gold coin – more than a peasant would earn in a lifetime. "Are you related to this child?" he asked gravely of the woman who comforted the boy.

She nodded, but it was an unnecessary question. Even Jack knew that. From the cast of the villagers' faces – their thin, pointed noses and watery blue eyes – it looked as if most of them were related.

"I am his aunt."

"Then this is for the child. When he is seven, he must be sent to Glastonbury Abbey. Will you swear to it?"

She nodded and turned the gold coin over in her grubby palm, awed. "I swear it."

Jack felt a confused rush of pride, and something more – sadness. He reflected on his own childhood as a foundling and on all the motherless children. Was his mother out in the world somewhere, waiting to claim him when the time was right?

Cedric himself heard the villagers' confessions, not trusting the peasant priest to help lift the stain upon their souls.

Rather than pray with the monks and lay brothers, Jack busied himself inspecting some of the village gardens. Cabbages, beans, onions, garlic, asparagus, parsley and peas had been planted in varying stages of growth in neat hummocks. The women worked with digging sticks and their children weeded carefully between the plants and pulled stones from the earth.

When he had exhausted the limited possibilities of the gardens, Jack wandered into a nearby meadow, where Lara could be seen, searching the surrounding woods for wild herbs and flowers to dye cloth.

"What is the lichen to be used for?" Jack asked, walking over to watch Lara tugging the plant life away from a stone.

"It will dye cloth violet." Lara held up a pouch. "In here I have gathered club moss to make green. Earlier we passed by some weld and I was itching to stop and pick it, for it makes a fine yellow. But I was in discussion with the abbot."

"I noticed."

Her eyebrows rose at the sourness in Jack's voice.

"What were you talking about?" he asked. A distant crash beneath the oaks and beeches turned into a fleeing deer and he swivelled to watch it.

"The scourge," Lara said flatly. "That it should not be used to harm innocent souls: midwives and healers, maids and widows without husbands, women who are bold enough to speak their own minds." She tugged a last bit of lichen from the rock. "We must return to the village. The abbot will surely have finished hearing confession by now. Then we can continue to Wells."

The rest of the journey continued without incident. Lara rode ahead beside Abbot Cedric's carriage and seemed to be engaged in intense conversation most of the way. If anyone thought it strange that a newly hired kitchen boy should be talking so freely to the abbot, no one commented. It was known that Abbot Cedric was saintly in his dealings with all men. It had even been said that he believed that, with the exception of the King, all men were equal.

Jack wished he could be riding alongside the abbot. Instead he was stuck at the back of the retinue, riding his pony alongside the cart that pulled the still-snoring kitchener, sprawled upon a sack of meal.

They passed through farmland where teams of

oxen dragged wooden ploughs through the claggy soil, ready for a final autumn planting. Men walked behind the plough and scattered grain, followed by a horse-drawn harrow that covered the grain over. Children danced in and out of the furrows to chase away the flocks of pigeons, rooks and crows that dived and swooped to peck up the exposed seed. Some of the boys pelted the crows with stones, but Jack noted that no one dared to harm a pigeon – those would belong to the Bishop of Bath and Wells, and to the church.

In the next village, where they stopped to fill their flasks with cool well water, one family was building walls for an animal enclosure. Together, men and women wove together strips of willow and then plastered and smeared it with an evil-smelling slurry of clay, chopped straw, dung and ox hair. They glanced up to gawk at the fine retinue of monks and just as swiftly bent their heads back to their labour.

Jack was used to hard work in Glastonbury Abbey's grand kitchen, but at least there was variety in his tasks and the chance to dream up and create new dishes, as well as opportunities to escape to the orchard and practise being a knight. But for villagers, he thought, as he watched women standing shin-deep in a freezing stream, carding wool

through spiked boards, life was endless drudgery –
performing the same boring, wearisome tasks over
and over again.

Jack drew in a sharp breath. The retinue had rounded
the final ridge of the Mendips. In the distance, two
towers rose proudly into the sky: Wells Cathedral!
Even from here, Jack could see the intricacy of the
nave's pointed spires and the procession of arches
that adorned the entire front, all glowing with reds,
blues and golds. He understood now why it was
said to have taken decades to complete – twice the
number of years most men could expect to live.

Jack waited, impatient to view the cathedral
from close up, while the abbot dismounted from his
carriage and knelt stiffly on the bare earth to pray.

CHAPTER 6

On Abbot Cedric's signal, they descended into the cathedral town of Wells. Jack was impressed to see a bustling market in a large square. There was a cheese stall, with great pan-shaped wheels of cheese, pig sellers, horse sellers, poultry sellers, goat and sheep sellers. The smell of livestock was familiar to Jack, but it was a bright, cloudless October day. He wondered what the market would be like during the winter – no doubt a quagmire of dung.

People called noisily to draw attention to their wares. A knife sharpener ran a blunted knife along the edge of a wet grindstone. Spice sellers babbled nonsense about the exotic lands their pepper, nutmeg, cloves, saffron and cinnamon came from – places teeming with dragons, goblins and kings who breathed fire.

Sharp-eyed peasant wives sat on crudely carved

stools guarding heaped pyramids of onions, cabbages and garlic. A foreign-looking man sold silk ribbons and bolts of fine cloth. These, Jack saw, were being fingered by women whose dresses were cleaner and of better quality than most of the motley throng around them.

A smithy stall sold knives, shears, needles, pots and pans. As they rode past, Jack assessed the quality of the cooking pots. They were thin-based, their surfaces black and pimpled from the forge, unlike the enormous pots and pans at Glastonbury, which were all scrubbed and burnished to a shine.

Abbot Cedric seemed to have little interest in or patience for the market. His carriage passed through it at a steady pace, with Lara still riding by his side. As they approached an old stone archway in the corner of the square, he spoke a few words to Lara, who then dropped behind to rejoin Jack.

Jack tried to be nonchalant, as though it were not a highly unusual privilege for a girl disguised as a kitchen boy to ride alongside the Abbot of Glastonbury for an entire day's journey. Jealousy pricked at him like a swarm of biting ants. Until the previous night, when Jack had roused him from prayer, Abbot Cedric had barely noticed him.

A commotion ahead of them at the gate woke

Jack from these bitter thoughts. Curt words were promising to become an argument as shaved monks, armed with weapons that made them seem more like soldiers than men of God, argued with Abbot Cedric's chamberlain.

"Leave it alone, Wilfred," Abbot Cedric called to his chamberlain from his carriage. Then he personally addressed the guards: "I am the Abbot of Glastonbury. If you refuse entrance, your master will be most displeased."

"There will be no speaking with my master if we don't let you in," the head gatekeeper sneered, with an insolence that made Jack gasp. "The bishop has ordered that no visitor is to have entrance to the cathedral while there is still the threat of plague."

Abbot Cedric's voice turned low and quiet. "I ask you one last time, Brother, for entrance. If you refuse, I cannot vouch for the consequences to you."

His words seemed to have an effect, and the soldier monks drew away from the barred gate to hold a hasty conference. When they at last returned and opened the gate, Abbot Cedric drew himself up regally and passed through.

Following at the end of the retinue, Jack let his mouth fall open with awe at the sight that greeted him. The cathedral was magnificent. From rows of niches, hundreds of carved statues in bright pigments of red, blue, yellow, green and gold looked out at him. The rows were arranged with the statue of Christ at the top, then the apostles, saints, bishops and knights, all the way down to ground level where, given the absence of carvings, Jack assumed peasant worshippers belonged.

"Jack," Lara hissed, "we are going to the bishop's palace."

"Not into the cathedral?" Jack longed to see inside, especially the moon clock, which was famous throughout the West Country for marking the phases of the moon.

Reluctantly, he turned his pony to accompany the others to the bishop's palace, and Jack could not help but be impressed with the palace, too. It was a magnificent building, surrounded by a moat with four corner towers. Between two octagonal towers, a drawbridge had been lowered and the heavy metal portcullis raised, in contrast to the hostile treatment they had received at the market gate. White swans glided on the moat, creating a tranquil scene.

Inside was a thriving garden with orchards and vegetable and medicine gardens. Stable boys came forward to take the visitors' horses, ready to feed, water and stable them.

A monk led the abbot's party, including Jack and Lara, to the great hall. There they were asked to wait and left to idle their time away admiring grand paintings and ornate tapestries, some partially blackened by soot from the enormous hearth that stood at one end of the hall.

A good while later, a man swept in, accompanied by a bevy of monks. He was distinguished from his fellows by the fine cut of his tunic and hose and the jewel-encrusted bishop's mitre that crowned his head. His sharp black eyes travelled over the weary party and seemed to Jack to rest momentarily on Lara, before returning to the abbot.

"Robert Fox," murmured Abbot Cedric with a grave nod.

"*Bishop* Fox," Robert Fox corrected.

The abbot's brow furrowed, as if in confusion. "But I have come to see Bishop Benedictus."

Jack marvelled at hearing this lie. He wondered who would be high enough to hear Abbot Cedric's confession.

Robert Fox was momentarily caught off guard. "You have not heard then?"

"Heard?"

"Bishop Benedictus returned from the Holy Lands only to meet a most terrible and tragic end."

Abbot Cedric's gaze did not waver. "What was the cause of my friend's death?"

Robert Fox also did not look away. His voice lowered. "He had brought back the plague. You are brave coming here at this time, my friend."

"And those who tended him?"

"Dead," answered Robert Fox sharply. He twisted his mouth into a smile. "But come, Abbot. This is not a subject to be discussed before servants. We will repair to the solar."

"I cannot see why the death of the Bishop of Bath and Wells should be a matter of secrecy . . ."

Jack saw that Robert Fox shifted on his feet, his hand unconsciously reaching to the right side of his tunic just above his hip – the place from which a knight might draw a sword.

"Why is it that no news was sent to me?" Abbot Cedric demanded.

"It was an oversight. I will find out which of my clerics is responsible and he will be punished, I assure you."

"And the funeral?"

"I am sorry that you have not arrived in time," said Fox, looking anything but sorry. "He was buried yesterday."

Abbot Cedric did not disguise his astonishment.

"What! No proper funeral, with other bishops, the priests, the King?"

"There was no chance for any display," replied Fox. "We could not allow the body to spread its pestilence." There was a short pause before he added, "The King has been informed and will not travel to Wells while there is risk of the Black Death to him and his courtiers."

Jack blanched at the thought of the plague's hideous black buboes blossoming beneath people's armpits. He was no stranger to skinning hares and daily plunged his hands into the carcasses of animals, but the horrors of illness made him squeamish. At the abbey, he had once heard the monk in charge of the infirmary say that buboes needed to be cut for the disease to leave the body. A mixture of tree resin, lily roots and dried human dung must then be put on the cuts as a paste.

"The King has agreed that I should act as regent," Robert Fox finished, with undisguised triumph.

"And the bishop's will?" enquired the abbot.

"It has not been found."

"But when it is found . . ."

Robert Fox bowed his head to hide his irritation. "I am regent until then," he hissed, in a way that made Jack flinch so noticeably that Lara turned to him in enquiry. It had been almost dark in the woods beneath the tor, but Jack recognised that sibilant sound. Robert Fox was the man who had chased Lara's grandmother!

Jack and Lara were directed to unpack the kitchen cart with the help of William, a smiling lad from the bishop's kitchen. Lara was reluctant and said plainly to Jack that she would only continue to keep up her kitchen boy pretence until she had learned where her grandmother was being imprisoned.

Jack, however, felt a surge of excitement at the opportunity to work in another kitchen and learn its secrets. He surveyed the bustling palace kitchen with its long rows of pots and pans and kettles hanging from sturdy iron hooks. It was at least as grand as the abbey kitchen and he wondered if Abbot Cedric had committed the sin of pride by bringing his cook with him.

Jack breathed in the familiar odours of woodfire mingled with cooked onions, roasting meat and something sweeter – mint perhaps. He felt relieved to be in a place he knew well, a place where he belonged. He loved the busy industry, the furious chopping and whisking, even the ill-tempered curses of people darting back and forth to ensure the bread had risen, the meat was not burned and the egg pudding did not sink. It made him feel alive. Working with others to create a magnificent meal that would be eaten with pleasure and never repeated filled him with satisfaction.

Spit boys, their skin permanently red from their nearness to the fire, cranked iron handles to turn the oily carcasses of boars and enormous slabs of venison over the flames. People carted baskets and crates of food back and forth. Servants scrubbed pots with their arms plunged up to their armpits in scalding water. Others scraped the burned pot bottoms with sand and ash.

Cooks armed with lethally sharp knives reduced carrots, onions and other vegetables to neatly chopped piles. Others whisked eggs, thickened almond-meal sauces or sat on crude stools plucking the feathers from geese, partridges, capons, swans and peacocks.

Kitchener Payne had now awoken and found his way to the kitchen. After establishing that he had slept for the entire journey, he bawled at Jack and Lara for not waking him, then introduced himself to Master Simeon, the head cook at the bishop's palace, and asked where the cellar was. He would soon be down there drinking from the wine barrels, thought Jack, like a pig at a trough.

Master Simeon gestured with annoyance in the direction of the cellar and stalked back to supervise the preparations for a feast. Word had come to the kitchen that an important guest had arrived. Before Brother Payne could waddle down to the cellar, however, a servant bearing a tray with two richly jewelled goblets and a flask of wine passed by.

Long accustomed to the laxness of the abbey's kitchen under his rule, Brother Payne openly grabbed the flask and took a swig. The servant stared, shocked, but was too frightened to protest.

Jack felt proud that Abbot Cedric's importance was being acknowledged, but the notion of a feast sat uneasily with him. Was it appropriate to hold a feast when, only days before, the Bishop of Bath and Wells had died of the plague?

Master Simeon saw Jack gawping at Brother Payne. "Get to work, boy," he growled. "We will need every hand we can get. You look stupid, but even a simpleton can make a decent apple sauce.

"And the other boy," he continued, pointing now at Lara, who had started to shrink away. "You will help make the coffins for the custard."

Although Lara nodded, Jack could see that,

beneath her red fringe, tangled now in the steam of the kitchen, her eyes were mutinous.

Jack groaned at the simplicity of his work. He would like to be slivering and gilding the calves' heads, or even steaming the asparagus and whisking a sauce from egg yolks, parsley and cream. Instead he was skinning an entire barrel of apples, creating long, snake-like peelings. He chopped the apples finely, added honey and searched the clay pots of spices for some cinnamon to set off the tart apple flavour.

At a distant bench, he could see Lara grimly rolling pastry. She wielded the rolling pin like a weapon. Jack could tell she was itching to be free to find her grandmother. He hung the pot of apples over the coals and stirred until the fruit had turned to mush. When it was sufficiently cool, he strained the sauce until it was perfectly smooth.

His task complete, Jack hastened to join Lara. Brother Payne was occupied and Master Simeon, who was shouting at a poor spit boy who had allowed the mutton to become dry, was too busy to notice.

Lara had finished making the pastry coffins and was now candying rose petals and leaves, rosemary flowers and marigolds. She dissolved isinglass powder with rose water then stirred in blanched almonds crushed fine by the kitchen boy, William, with a heavy pestle. Lara added powdered sugar and cream and beat them together while William used almond oil to grease wooden moulds in the shapes of rabbits and woodcocks. Measuring nothing, Lara poured in as much or little of each ingredient as she seemed to feel was right.

Jack was grudgingly impressed by her deft touch. "Who taught you to cook?" he asked. If William thought it strange that one kitchen boy should ask this of another, he showed no sign of it.

"My grandmother. As a girl, she worked for a time in the palace kitchens." Mischievously, Lara then added, "She thought cooking fine work for a boy."

William's cheeks flushed with eager agreement. "My own grandmother was well pleased on the day I came here from our village. She said that, even if I had to be a spit boy, it would be like being a prince after coming from the cruck. Though I am still up at sunrise and never in bed till after dark, I am warm and well fed. My poor brothers must work in the rain and mud with only a pottage of peas and salt bacon to eat."

"And how long have you been working here in the kitchen?" Jack asked. His eyes narrowed with disapproval as William tore roughly at the delicate rose petals.

"One week," confessed William.

"One week!"

"It is like that for all of us in the kitchen," said William, defensive now. "It is how I got my opportunity. All who worked for the old bishop were driven away. His Lordship, Bishop Fox, wanted new staff for his household. He said he wished to sweep it clean with a new broom."

"He got rid of the house servants as well?" asked Jack, astonished.

William nodded. "The only one who has remained is Master Simeon. He came to work here before the old bishop returned and lived here a full month on the moon clock before any of us."

"Boys!"

Jack jumped as the firelight dimmed and a shadow loomed. Master Simeon was gazing down at them, his thin lips pressed together. "William, you will turn the spits and you two . . ." he pointed to Lara and Jack, "you will tend your master cook, who is ill."

CHAPTER 7

Brother Payne lifted his fat head, retched, then lowered it again to vomit into the wooden pail behind the barn.

Jack could not feel sorry for him. This was not the first time the kitchener's binges had ended in sickness. How was it possible that Abbot Cedric did not see what a drunken, lazy fool his master cook was? Did he not see or did he not *want* to see? Occasionally, Brother Payne had slurred some sentimental and self-important nonsense about a Crusade and how the abbot would always be in debt to him.

"Do you think we should help him?" Jack whispered doubtfully.

Lara nodded as if it pained her to do so. "I can fetch some herbs from the medicine garden. Though, from the look of his vomit, he needs to chew charcoal to settle his stomach. Then I'll make a brew from golden seal and thyme for his headache."

Jack fetched some charcoal. It was not burned-down wood from the grate, but proper charcoal brought in by the charcoal burners. He had sometimes seen the charcoal burners in Glastonbury at work near the edge of the woods. They had stacked an enormous heap of timber and then covered it with earth. Once the heap was set alight, the hardest thing, according to one of the lay brothers who worked with Jack, was to avoid going to sleep and letting it burn out of control. For two to three nights at a stretch, the charcoal burner watched over the smouldering mound, sitting upon a small wooden stool with only one leg so that he would fall if he started to sleep.

"Eat this, Brother Payne," said Jack, pushing a lozenge of charcoal into the monk's blubbery, vomit-flecked mouth.

The kitchener groaned and spat it out. "I'm dying," he choked.

Lara returned with a handful of herbs. "Did he chew on the charcoal?"

Jack shook his head. "I think this may be something worse than usual. I have never seen him so sick."

The kitchener had started to rave, his face slick with sweat. "Put down the cheese," he cried. "No, I cannot see the goblet." He thrashed about. "The cat is in the cupboard."

Lara felt the monk's face. "It is more than fever, I think." Turning aside, she whispered, "I fear he has been poisoned."

"Poisoned!"

"Sssh!"

Jack looked around guiltily and was thankful that a cart laden with straw had just gone trundling past, masking his cry.

"What? Who?"

Lara looked thoughtful. "From his fever and madness, I would guess poisonous toadstools."

This time Jack knew to keep his voice low. "Someone has used toadstools to poison him?"

"It is only a guess. I wish Grandmother were here – she would know for certain."

"Your grandmother knows about poison?" The instant he said it, Jack wished it unsaid.

Lara rounded on him, eyes blazing. "Grandmother knows what every decent healer must know, kitchen boy. Poisoning is the other side of healing, as dark is to light. We must know the properties of plants so that we can use them wisely and well."

Jack swallowed. He felt like a clumsy dolt.

"And," Lara added fiercely, "if you pride yourself on cooking, then you should know all the properties of herbs. Otherwise you will be like every other peasant in the West Country – a servant to people who would prefer you did not think for yourself!"

"I'm sorry," said Jack, stung into apology. "I didn't mean to suggest your grandmother . . ." He trailed off as William came racing out from the kitchen, clearly looking for somebody.

Lara rolled her eyes. "Wait by the kitchener," she said to Jack. "I will be back as soon as I am able."

It was a long and terrible wait. The monk groaned and thrashed on straw soaked through with vomit and sweat.

When Lara returned, it was with a small flask rather than the fistful of green leaves Jack had come to expect from her. "This will help counter some of the toadstool poisoning," she said. "Help me open his mouth."

Jack struggled to prise open his master's lips, now gleaming with drool. He felt the bite of blunt, yellowed teeth on his fingers. "Hurry."

Carefully, Lara dispensed a number of drops.

"Will he be all right?" In his heart of hearts, Jack was uncertain whether he wanted the kitchener to live.

Lara nodded. "I think so. But we need to talk," she murmured. "Not here, though. Give me a bishop's ruby ring if I'm wrong, but the walls here have many eyes and ears."

With Brother Payne collapsed on a pile of straw, Jack felt a great surge of guilt and elation – he was truly free. He and Lara passed through the gate easily enough by claiming they had been sent to purchase spices from the marketplace.

But the market's invigorating hustle and bustle now felt hollow to Jack. The bright smiles of the peasant women and traders hawking their wares seemed to have an undercurrent of desperation.

"My grandmother and I sometimes set up a stall here," Lara said.

"What did you sell?" Jack was curious about everything Lara said or did. How was it that she was so knowledgeable about herbs for medicine and poison, religion, politics and making rabbit and woodcock moulds from sugar paste? Just once he wished he could show her that he was good at something, too.

"Whatever we found on our travels," Lara said. "Things that we had traded for – ribbons, beads, toys, spoons. People would sometimes ask Grandmother to tell them their futures, for she has a gift of seeing."

"She told me my future!" Jack exclaimed. "On top of the tor! I didn't ask her, she just did."

Lara nodded. "Grandmother is never wrong." Then she added in a muttered undertone, "That is why he has captured her."

The cathedral bells had started to peal. It seemed to Jack that this was not a fit mourning for the old bishop's death; the bells had a triumphant, almost celebratory tone.

As the noise grew more deafening, Lara pulled Jack into a winding street edged with tall, narrow houses painted bright red or blue and black and smelling of tar and linseed oil. Here, they were partly sheltered from the noise of the marketplace and the bells.

"We must devise a plan to rescue Grandmother," Lara said. "I asked in the market earlier and there has been no public burning, except of a young woman who served as a maid in the bishop's palace. Robert Fox would be sure to make Grandmother's death a public spectacle. That means she is still imprisoned, and I would lay my heart on her being held in the bishop's dungeons. It will take all our cunning to free her."

Jack backed away. "What do you mean by *we*?"

"Aren't you going to help me?"

"No," Jack blurted.

Knights always offer assistance to damsels in distress.

Seeing her stricken expression, he amended this to, "I mean . . . I don't . . . it's too dangerous."

Lara turned away from him and an uncomfortable silence fell.

Knights are always courageous in the face of danger.

"Well," Jack said finally. "What would it involve?"

Lara's radiant smile was greater reward than a purse of gold. Jack almost felt like a real knight. "We need to find a way to get into the dungeon," she said. "Then we can trick the guard into giving us the key so that we can smuggle Grandmother out."

Jack felt ill. This would be no easy feat. He thought about Kitchener Payne, convulsed and vomiting into the soiled straw; the bishop's palace was a dangerous place.

"Who poisoned Brother Payne?" he wondered

aloud. "What do we know he has eaten or drunk since yesterday? We know he took your sleeping brew."

Lara glared at him. "Don't be stupid. You saw what I put into it."

Jack shook his head. "I'm not accusing you. I'm just pointing out that the only thing he has had since then was . . ."

"The wine," Lara finished.

"The one with the fancy goblets," Jack agreed. "Wine intended for fine company."

Lara nodded slowly. "For Abbot Cedric . . . Served on the master's orders?"

"We must warn the abbot before it is too late!" Jack exclaimed, adding quickly, "Before we rescue your grandmother."

A knight is loyal to his lady and his king.

Lara nodded, though it was clearly an effort.

"It will be difficult to talk with him unnoticed," Jack pointed out. "We'll have to think of some way to gain his attention without arousing the suspicion of Robert Fox's servants."

He was half-dreading that Lara would suggest swimming the moat, scaling the palace walls and squeezing through the abbot's slit windows, so it was a relief when she replied, "We'll return to the palace and request to see Abbot Cedric on a delicate kitchen matter."

As they hurried back through the market, the cathedral bells pealed again. "Abbot Cedric will be attending the service," Jack said to Lara.

Lara looked doubtful. "We only arrived a few hours ago."

"Trust me," Jack said. "When it comes to services and prayer, he's like clockwork."

CHAPTER 8

They entered the cathedral through a beautifully carved porch, then scurried through the doors on the western front into the nave. There Jack paused to stare up. Clusters of fluted pillars soared to the arched ceilings, some of which were richly painted. The tops of the pillars were carved with scenes of daily and religious life.

Lara pointed to a carving of a peasant with a toothache and Jack grimaced. It reminded him of the time he had been advised by the abbey's infirmary monk to burn a candle near his wisdom tooth to cause the worms gnawing beneath it to drop out. Later, a visiting tooth-puller prised the sore tooth from its socket in a pulp of enamel chips and blood. He had not been able to chew meat for weeks.

Deep in the cathedral, a service was taking place. Monks lined the choir stalls and Jack wondered how many secretly kneeled against the small carved shelves or benches – the misericords – that gave the impression they were still standing.

Though he had grown up in one of England's finest abbeys and attended more services than he would ever be able to count, the singing of the hymns never failed to move Jack. Deep, resonant voices rose with a swell of hope that went far beyond the awful drudgery of existence and became a pure cry to something much bigger than Jack felt he would ever understand. The oblates who had not yet become men accompanied them with their pure sopranos, weaving and soaring through the air like larks in full-throated song.

Abbot Cedric was deep in prayer, with his retinue of monks kneeling on the cold stone floor behind. A monk approached Lara and Jack with a forbidding expression.

"Come!" Lara tugged Jack into the shadows and they darted behind columns and along the wall until they reached shelter in the north cross-section. Above them, set into an arch, was the moon clock. Its maker, Peter Lightfoot, was said to have once been a monk at Glastonbury Abbey. Now Jack could see why it was so famous.

Above the clock, a puppet-like figure sat blank-faced and stiff-legged in a little crenellated tower. The clock beneath was comprised of three rings: a sun and moon revolving around the fixed centre of the Earth. The outermost of the three rings was marked with Roman numerals for the hours of the day. A golden sun moved around the numbers to show the current hour. In the middle ring, a silver star pointed to one of sixty Arabic numerals that represented the minutes. The innermost ring featured a small moon pointing to the current phase of the moon.

"Three days until dark moon," Lara said.

Jack nodded. Here was a fine clock to keep the months and to let the peasants know the right times for planting, and pilgrims the best time to set off for pilgrimage so that they could take advantage of the bright light of a fat moon.

The silver star moved from the fifty-ninth minute and the gold sun swung about to strike the hour of three. In the same instant, the little man in the tower struck the bell sharply with his hammer: one, two, three times, turning his head as if to listen to the sound.

As he did so, four figures emerged from a platform at the top of the clock. Jack recognised them from their painted armour: two knights and two Saracens. As they circled in a jousting tournament, one Saracen was tilted and knocked down.

Jack turned to Lara. "It's a wonder!"

Lara's own smile was grudging. "Grandmother says that the hours and minutes on the clock will come to rule us against our own better interests and wishes."

Jack shrugged. Living at the abbey, he was used to things happening by the clock. The monks went to services every three hours, starting with vigils, then matins, prime, tierce, sext, nones, vespers and complines. In the kitchen, Jack helped prepare bread and cheese for them to break their fast and then a proper dinner at noon, followed by a light supper when the daylight was gone and those who worked in the fields, or needed the light of the sun for their labours, had returned to shelter.

"The little man in the tower with the blank face –" he began.

"He looks a bit like you," Lara said.

Jack started to protest, then saw she was joking and gave her a friendly punch on the arm as if she were a real boy. "Who is he?"

"His name is Jack Blandiver," said a voice from behind them. "As for his identity, no one knows."

Jack spun around and was relieved to see a monk whose soft, gentle face suggested he wasn't going to growl at them. Rather, he looked up at the moon clock with wonder, mingled with something else . . . sadness.

"And the knights and Saracens?" Jack asked.

"Ah. That's an easier one," the monk replied. "The knights are our own good Crusaders who fight the Saracens for the Holy Land."

"More like the Saracens are fighting to keep their homeland," Lara muttered so that Jack alone could hear.

The monk continued to gaze at the clock face. "When Bishop Benedictus returned from the Holy Land, before he became ill, God rest his soul, this was where he spent time in deep thought, praying for the Crusaders and even the Saracens. It is said that the clock stopped at the moment of his death and it was a full minute before it started again."

The thought of Crusaders made Jack greedy for adventure. It would be thrilling to travel, first by ship, then by horse or camel or lion or dragon or whatever other outlandish creatures populated those foreign parts. He would travel as a knight with a grand herald and perhaps carry a lady's colours – his mother's colours – and he would bring back precious relics to Glastonbury Abbey. He imagined Abbot Cedric's sweet smile of thanks . . .

Abbot Cedric! They had to speak with him before he was poisoned!

When the nones service ended, Abbot Cedric and his monks set out for the bishop's palace.

Jack and Lara darted from the shadows and followed them.

"Abbot Cedric," Jack called, just as the abbot was about to step out of the cathedral.

The abbot turned in surprise. "Young Jack No Name."

"Abbot Cedric, sir. Kitchener Payne sent me to you regarding an issue of seasoning."

"Heavens, boy! Surely that is something for a cook to decide."

"Sir!" Lara cried. "It is more than that . . . Brother Payne has drunk himself into a stupor. He is incapable."

Now anger crept into the saintly Cedric's face. "Excuse me, Brothers," he said, excusing himself from his followers, then marched over to Jack and Lara. "Walk with me," he said in a crisp undertone that made Jack shiver.

When they had wandered far enough to escape being overheard, Jack burst out, before the abbot could berate them, "Kitchener Payne has been poisoned."

"What? This is absurd! Who would wish to poison my cook?"

"The poison wasn't intended for your cook, Abbot," Lara said quietly. "It was intended for you."

The abbot paused for a moment. "What makes you think so?"

"He drank wine from a flask being carried through the kitchen with two fine goblets," Jack said. "They were covered with rubies and emeralds."

Lara nodded in agreement. "Finer by far than common drinking cups. Too fine for anyone short of a bishop and his honoured guest."

"And the poison?" the abbot whispered, looking around him now, as if the carved, painted figures upon the church building might suddenly open their eyes and waggle their ears.

"I believe toadstools, sir," Lara said. "I gave him a remedy and for now he sleeps."

"And you suspect?"

At this, Lara and Jack remained silent. To suspect was one thing; to accuse a figure as powerful as Robert Fox was another and might well result in torture or death for them both.

Abbot Cedric seemed to see all of this in their

frightened faces. "I ask only for your suspicions, and they will not travel further than me. I must know for the safety of us all."

Lara began, "Robert –"

"Fox," Jack finished in a blaze of chivalry. If trouble *were* to result from the airing of their suspicions, then he would not let it fall upon Lara alone.

Abbot Cedric sighed and ran a hand through his silver hair, passing lightly over the shaved pate.

"What will you do?" Lara asked after a long silence.

"I will return to the palace," the abbot declared. "Now, more than before, I believe that Bishop Benedictus has met with an evil end."

"But, sir!" Jack protested. "If you go back, your life is in grave danger."

Abbot Cedric turned blazing blue eyes upon him. "My life on Earth," he corrected. "At times, I would dearly welcome the trumpets of heaven."

"Not now, though," said Lara tartly. "Not while there is Robert Fox in the bishopric. Not while there is the scourge. If you lose your life now, Abbot, there will be hundreds more who will be forced to give theirs with no such willingness."

The abbot nodded. "You are right. I will announce

that I am embarking on a fast. You two alone will be permitted to bring me tea and gruel and perhaps some of those candied roses . . ."

Jack was shocked.

The abbot's eyes twinkled. "Be assured, Jack, that I will confess my greed. I ask also that you be my eyes and ears among the servants and lay brothers."

"My grandmother, Abbot," Lara reminded him. "She must be freed immediately. I cannot afford to spend time being your eyes and ears."

"Robert Fox will not harm her while I am here. And if the bishop's will is found, or if we can prove it was poison and not plague that killed my friend, then I promise you, young lady, the scourge will end. It is best this way rather than risk *your* lives in a foolhardy attempt at rescue. The bishop's palace is guarded like a fortress."

Something had been niggling at Jack. "What if the will was destroyed?"

Abbot Cedric considered this. "Bishop Benedictus was a cautious man, though evidently not cautious enough. But I would lay my life . . ." and here he met Lara's bright eyes. "Yes, that life I seemed ready to give away so easily just now, that he has made a copy and hidden it."

CHAPTER 9

Jack kept his eyes peeled as they trudged back to the bishop's palace to check on the kitchener. There seemed to be a thousand nooks and crannies – large pots, newly turned earth, storage barrels and jars – a thousand places to hide a will.

Brother Payne was on the way to recovery and Jack and Lara enlisted the help of William to drag him to a small pallet in an abandoned animal enclosure. As they returned to the kitchen, Jack asked William, "What is your master like?"

By master, he had meant Robert Fox and was mildly surprised to hear William whisper, "Master Simeon is not greatly liked. He fines any of us who taste as we cook, even when it is to tell if a soup has been over-salted. He keeps close check on the cellar and allows us to drink only well water. Mother was told that Benedictus' cook let the workers drink ale and allowed the spit boys to take turns so that none was too badly burned. He even permitted the kitchen hands first pickings from the scraps before they were fed to the bishop's hounds!"

Jack made a faint sound of approval, as if he were equally impressed. Back at Glastonbury Abbey, he had had to put up with horrible Kitchener Payne, with his piggy eyes and wheezy, reeking breath, and not forgetting the wet rope he kept by the door. Yet the brother's drunkenness had meant that Jack and the fifty or so others who worked in the kitchens could taste as they worked and drink ale, too. Though he was only a boy, the other lay brothers deferred to Jack's decisions. They, like Abbot Cedric, falsely regarded him as Brother Payne's mouthpiece – as if, with every suggestion, he was only voicing the great cook's instructions!

"Why do you think Master Fox dismissed the other servants?" Lara asked, direct as always.

William shrugged. "The palace was in a great upheaval when the old bishop died. Perhaps the new bishop thought to sweep with a new broom."

"Like the scourge," Lara muttered.

Jack jumped in hastily to divert attention from Lara's words. "How did the bishop die?" he asked, this time remembering to make his face slightly stupid, as though he were simply a servant avid for more gossip.

"They say it was from the bishop's travel in the Holy Lands," William said, eager to oblige. "The plague had caught hold of him. The master ordered that no one was to see him except the leech, lest he spread the infection."

Jack and Lara exchanged a look.

"And no one else saw him?" Lara pressed.

"Only the maid," William said. "She tended the bishop and changed his linen." At the mention of the bed, another thought occurred to him. "It is said that the bishop's bed has no straw but a goose-down mattress! It has carved pillars and curtains with gold stars and silver moons and can sleep ten men!"

Jack could see why William – who no doubt bedded down on rushes in the great hall with the rest of the servants – was awed, but he was far more eager to learn about the maid. "Where is the maid now?" he asked.

William frowned. "Mary? She was locked in a cell, lest she spread the illness. The day before the bishop's funeral, she was burned as a witch."

Jack saw the whiteness of Lara's face and the tight lines of anger around her mouth. Before she could betray them, he jumped in. "Is the leech still about?"

The kitchen boy shook his head. "He was a travelling man. Soon after the bishop's death, they say he vanished from the palace."

"What? No one saw him leave?" Lara asked sharply.

William looked troubled, as if, above all, he wished to help. "The stable boys might know," he said. "You could try asking John. He is a cousin of my mother."

Jack and Lara slunk towards the stables.

"We will pretend we are enquiring about our ponies," Lara said. "I will say that mine was limping and I fear lameness."

A stable boy stacking dung that would be taken in cartloads to fertilise the fields told them where to find Master John. He was grooming a fine black horse in one of the stalls. Even if the stallion hadn't been snorting and pawing at the ground, Jack would have recognised the horse that nearly knocked him down on Glastonbury Tor.

"Master John?"

The man, middle-aged and heavy-set, looked up and grunted. "What do you want?"

"The kitchen boy, William, sent us."

At the mention of William's name, Master John softened. "Aye. Is he having trouble in the kitchen then? I promised his mother I'd keep an eye out for him."

"No trouble," Lara said. "I told him I was worried for my pony and he said to come to you for advice. She trod on something sharp."

"What's she like?"

"Russet, stout, with a sly humour."

At this, John grinned. "I know the one. But I assure you she is alive *and* kicking. The bruise on one of my boys' backsides will vouch for that."

"Do you know all the horses that come and go from the bishop's palace then?" Lara asked.

Master John nodded. "As if they were people."

"Are the horses like their owners?"

"Do you kick and bite?"

Lara laughed before she spoke again, this time lowering her pitch, as if remembering to be the kitchen boy she was impersonating. "I mean do they have similar temperaments. The plodding priest with the plodding pony. The quick-tempered man with the fiery stallion. The medical leech with the sly steed that's always wheedling for a meal."

Master John laughed. "You've hit the mark there. See that horse?" He pointed to a fat bay gelding devouring a load of straw. "That is a leech's steed."

"The leech's horse is still here then?" blurted Jack.

Master John looked at them more sharply. "Why do you ask?"

Lara sought to rescue the conversation. "Our master cook is ill and we need a leech. And not just any leech," she added. "We need a reputable one that the bishop himself might employ."

Master John shook his head. "I know nothing of that. All I can tell you is, a leech came here on this greedy horse and he has not yet come back to retrieve it."

"So the leech is still in the bishop's palace?" Jack pressed.

The stable man gestured towards the fat gelding. "Unless he has left his horse behind! And a fine horse it is, too."

"Our master will be most pleased to learn it," Lara said.

Kitchener Payne no longer vomited and seemed over the worst of the poisoning, though he continued to grunt and groan like a swine on the soiled straw pallet. Jack stood watching him for a while. As far as he was concerned, the longer the master cook remained indisposed, the better. They could use his illness as a reason to ask after the leech. The man had attended the bishop at his deathbed and would know the true symptoms of his malady.

Jack followed Lara's sharp gaze across the courtyard to a party of black-robed monks wearing the badge of Robert Fox, a red fox pursuing a white dove. Some of the monks carried pikes and swords – the weapons of knights, not men of God!

"What is it?" he whispered to Lara.

She wrapped her thin arms tight around her tunic. "A hunting party."

"At this time?" asked Jack, surprised. Days after the death of a bishop hardly seemed the right moment for revelries such as a hunt.

Lara's face was so white he could see blue veins at her temples. "They are hunting for witches." An array of conflicting emotions passed across her face, ending in a flush of fury. "I don't care what the abbot says. We must find Grandmother. She is the one who will know best how to stop this. She will tell us what to do."

Then why didn't she do it before? Jack was loyal to the abbot, as a knight to his lord. He did not want to disobey Abbot Cedric's orders. How could he help

Lara and the abbot at the same time?

Lara began to tap one worn, wooden-soled shoe on the cobbles.

"I will help you free her from the dungeon," Jack said finally. "But then you must flee, and I will stay to serve the abbot and be his eyes and ears, as he commanded."

Lara nodded. "Will you swear it?"

Jack felt a flush of fear and pride. He had always wished to make an oath just like a knight. He knelt in the muck and tried to imagine Lara in a beautiful silk gown with a horned hat and gossamer headdress rather than a rough brown tunic spattered with food stains. "I swear," he murmured, "on God, the King and my own life that I will help you, Lady."

Jack had half-expected her to punch him on the arm or laugh outright. Instead, he was surprised to see Lara regarding him solemnly.

"I will accept your help and am grateful for it."

"How do you think we will do it?" asked Jack. "We can't just go down to the dungeon and demand her release. There will be guards."

At Lara's disgusted expression, he continued hurriedly, "At the very least we should attempt it when the monks are at prayer. They pray every three hours. The next service will be vespers."

"We should go to the cathedral and check the time."

Jack nodded, though he already knew the time. It lived inside his body. After a lifetime spent in an abbey, where every element of the day was governed by time, it was second nature to him. Time to pray, time to work, time to pray, time to serve breakfast, lunch and dinner. He said nothing, however, because he longed to return to the cathedral and, in particular, the marvellous moon clock.

"And then we will return to the kitchen," continued Lara. "I have in mind a most effective meal . . ."

This time, Jack was too nervous to be awed by the beauty of the cathedral's soaring arches and carvings. When they reached the moon clock, they found they were just in time to see the hand moving to point to the hour of five.

There was a whirr. Jack Blandiver in his tower above struck a bell with his hammer. On cue, two knights and two Saracens emerged from a little building at the top of the clock.

Jack watched, fascinated, as one of the knights struck a Saracen. The Saracen went down stiffly, with a slight delay that Jack could not recall from his earlier visit. He wondered what had caused it. A fault in the mechanism? Something its maker, Peter Lightfoot, had not anticipated?

"They will go to vespers in one more hour," whispered Jack, though he could have told her that without seeing the moon clock.

"Good," Lara said. "That gives us time to concoct a very special dish."

CHAPTER 10

Jack stood beside Lara, grinding almonds and crumbling wheat bread to thicken the stew. Lara had said that the herbs must be well disguised. One in particular tasted bitter. He only hoped the guard wouldn't notice it.

No one had questioned their appearance in the kitchen or the fact that they had set themselves up at an oak bench and begun cooking. But it had been that way since their arrival. With their master cook absent, they were everybody's and nobody's servants. Still, to make certain they would not be challenged, Lara had announced loud enough for all to hear that their master had the gripe and he had entrusted his meals to them alone.

William had been kept busy, shelling peas then taking pots out into the courtyard to scrub with ash. On one of his return trips, however, Jack contrived to be near the entrance and bump into him. As he did so, he asked conversationally when the servants usually ate their meals.

"After the masters," William replied.

"There must be many mouths to feed. I have heard there are even dungeons here. So I suppose there must be dungeon guards to be fed as well?" said Jack, hating himself for his clumsiness. He was sure that Lara would have found a cleverer way of digging for information.

William smiled with the satisfaction of knowing more than this newcomer. "There is only one guard and he dines when the bell rings for the end of vespers."

"But who can be spared to take him his meal?" asked Jack.

"Master Simeon himself does it, after he has had his own," William said, seeming to wonder at the oddness of this even as he said it.

Jack secretly agreed. *Why would a master chef take it upon himself to deliver meals to a dungeon guard? Unless there was a secret he wished to be kept . . .*

Jack returned to Lara with this news and watched as she emptied another pouch of the mysterious bitter green herb into the pottage. "We must be swift," she murmured. "While Master Simeon dines, we will take this to the guard."

"How long will it take to work?" Jack asked.

"Not long," Lara assured him.

"Who will deliver it?" Jack asked.

The question had only just left his lips when Master Simeon suddenly loomed above them. He pointed to Lara. "You!"

Lara looked up bravely.

"Are you the boy who made the sugar moulds?"

She nodded.

"I wish you to make more." He pointed to the bench where she had earlier made the candied petals and sugared moulds. "Now!"

Holding the blazing torch in one hand and the pottage in the other, Jack crept through narrow stone passages and down steep stairs. The stone floor and walls were dank with seeping water and smelled of mould, burned candles and other, far less pleasant things. In the distance, Jack could hear the faintest echoes of something or someone moaning.

At the sound of Jack's wooden-soled boots ringing against the stone floor, the guard leapt to his feet. "Who's there?"

Jack made his eyes blank and his mouth stupid

before creeping forward. "I have come to bring your dinner, sir."

The guard surveyed him suspiciously in the orange glow of a flaming torch. "Where is Master Simeon?"

"I have come in his place," said Jack, and then, a hasty masterstroke: "Master Simeon was called to attend Bishop Fox."

"What is your name?"

Before he could think to lie, Jack replied, "Jack." He added hastily, "Here is your meal, sir."

The guard reached for the stew greedily and sniffed with appreciation. "This makes a change from bread and gravy."

Jack nodded, not daring to say more as the guard took a scoop with the wooden spoon and grunted with pleasure.

Someone moaned from further down the stone corridor, followed by a deeper male rumble.

The guard scowled. "Shut your hag face," he shouted, then, as if sensing Jack's stare, frowned. Jack made his eyes go blank once again. "Why are you lurking about like a runt after a bone? Get. Come back later for the pot."

Jack nodded hasty obedience and scrambled back up the passage. Lara had said the potion would work within a quarter of an hour. When he left the kitchen with the guard's pottage, saying it was for Kitchener Payne, she had been furiously mixing a bowl of sugar crystals.

If he hurried, he would only just have time to return to the cathedral and the moon clock. Something had been worrying him ever since they had left it.

The moon clock's face glowed in the last coloured rays of light filtering through the stained-glass windows. Its three rings each told a different sort of time. The time of hours: when to get the meals served, when to go to prayer, when the peasants might pause from their ceaseless toil for lunch. The time of minutes: when Payne would lose his patience at Jack's disappearances and wield that cursed wet rope, when that poor drowned village woman had breathed her last, when Lara's brew would finally take effect upon the guard. And moon time: when to plant new crops, when to set out upon a journey of pilgrimage or escape . . .

The sun hand turned to the hour. This time, Jack ignored the little puppet figure – Jack Blandiver – banging upon the bell with his hammer. Instead, he intently watched the chase between the knights and the Saracens. Again, there was a delay when the Saracen was tumbled with the pike. As if the mechanism were faulty or as if it had been interfered with . . .

With growing certainty, Jack knew that he must return to the abbot. He had something very important to tell him. But first, he would fetch Lara and help her to release her grandmother as he had sworn to do.

The earth pot lay in broken shards with the guard sprawled beside it, snoring. His pike lay where it had fallen.

Jack stepped over his body while Lara searched it with nimble fingers until she triumphantly brandished a set of iron keys on a ring.

They hurried along the dank corridor as far as the first cell. Jack gasped at the stench. He wanted to retch. Through the rusted grating in the cell door, Jack could just pick out a tiny ragged figure, nearly indistinguishable from the pile of soiled straw surrounding it. His torchlight revealed a wooden bucket in one corner that must be the source of the evil stink.

Lara turned a key in the lock and pushed her way into the cell. "Grandmother!" she moaned, seizing the bundle of rags in a fierce embrace. "What have they done to you?"

A low animal moan told them that, whatever it was, it had been cruel.

"We have to get her out of here," Lara cried. "Help me carry her. Help me!"

Jack hesitated, and not just because of the terrible smell. Though they had concocted a plan to get into the dungeon, they had given little thought to getting out again. How were they going to smuggle a broken old lady out of the bishop's palace past hundreds of servants, not to mention all the priests and monks swarming about?

From another cell came a hoarse male shout. "Help me. Do not leave me here, I beg you."

Jack turned to Lara and saw her lips tighten. "We cannot help any others," she said firmly. "It will be difficult enough getting Grandmother free."

"Please," the voice called. "I beg of you. Have mercy . . ."

Jack recognised the sense of Lara's words, but it twisted his heart to hear the raw terror in the man's voice. Grabbing the keys from the cell door, he continued along the corridor.

In the next stone cell, a large-framed man lay in the dirty straw. When he saw Jack's torchlight at the grating, he reached out his hand towards it, begging for help.

"Come," said Jack quickly, unlocking the door. "Can you walk?"

The man rose stiffly to his feet and nodded. "They have been more careful with me than her," he said in a hoarse voice, indicating the cell where Lara was helping her grandmother. "Curse Robert Fox," he muttered. "As for getting out of here – I have spent many long and terrible hours planning how I would escape if only someone would turn that wretched key. I believe there is a way . . ."

If he had thought he was going to vomit before, Jack now felt as if he could purge a year of meals from his lurching stomach. But he swallowed hard, took the weight of one side of Lara's softly moaning grandmother, and followed the man through one shadowy stone passage and then another. At last they came to a large wooden bench with two holes carved into it for two guards to sit together as they toileted.

"We can lift this," said the man, "and the lady and

I will travel down and along the sewer to where it empties into the moat. Can you swim, boy?"

Jack nodded, grateful now for the summer hours stolen from the kitchen to teach himself to swim like the other village boys – first in the fast-moving shallows, then in the deep pools. But they had been clear and free of the odiferous, brownish-green scum on the bishop's palace moat.

"And you?" the man asked Lara.

She nodded curtly.

Gently, the man took her grandmother's arm from Lara and nodded at Jack to let her go. Then he stepped up against her, propping her up like a broken puppet.

"Then you can meet us on the other side of the palace walls when night falls and be prepared to help me ferry her across the moat if it is needed?"

Lara nodded, exhausted. "We will."

Alarmed, Jack realised that he was being included in the flight from the palace. "No! I cannot help any further. I must return to the abbot."

The man's thick black eyebrows rose. "When the guard is discovered or wakes, the alarm will be raised."

With a sinking heart, Jack recalled that he had told the guard his name. It would be very easy for

Fox and his followers to put it all together: the special stew, their questioning of William . . .

And no one lied under threat of . . . what? What methods would they use to question him? His stomach contracted with fear. But he must see the abbot. Would it somehow be possible to tell him of his discovery before they left?

"You said that Master Simeon brings the guard his meal after vespers," interrupted Lara urgently. "We don't have much time, Jack. We're racing against the clock."

As he sprinted back up towards the courtyard, Jack didn't dare to pause for breath, though his lungs were on fire. When they were close to the door, Lara called after him. "Wait a moment. Regain your breath or it will look strange to the guards at the gate."

Outside, Jack spotted William crossing the courtyard and hurried over. William grinned at the sight of him.

"William, I . . ." Jack racked his brain to think of a way he could get William to take a message to the abbot without betraying either of them. "Would you be so kind as to deliver a message to Abbot Cedric from me? It is a private matter and must be spoken to him when he is alone."

William's grin faded and he nodded fearfully.

Jack's words were measured. "Will you please tell the abbot exactly these words: his kitchen servant, Jack Blandiver, is very sorry for mooning around and must find the will to keep better time."

Jack repeated the words, then made William repeat them back to him. He hoped he was not being too clever or too obtuse. Would the abbot understand that it was a riddle to be solved? Abbot Cedric might dismiss it as utter nonsense, but Jack hoped he would consider it more closely when the alarm was raised and he and Lara were nowhere to be found.

Jack hurried back to where Lara was pretending to busy herself fetching water from one of the courtyard wells.

The bells pealed for the end of vespers just as they reached the palace's arched gate. The guards had already begun to turn the enormous wheel to wind up the drawbridge.

"Stop! We wish to go out," Jack cried.

A guard looked at him coolly, the red fox badge on his habit glinting in the purple-toned dusk. "What is your business beyond the bishop's palace this night?"

Jack's tongue twisted into knots, but Lara rushed in, cool as an autumn breeze. "We have been sent by Master Simeon with the holy well water to the bakehouse, so that the bread may be blessed at the beginning of Bishop Fox's reign."

The guard looked pleased. "It is a very fine thing for Wells that a bishop of such righteous strength now rules."

They lowered the drawbridge again and Lara and Jack, with their pail of well water, darted out into the thickening shadows.

"Where will we hide?" Jack demanded, once they were in the marketplace and out of the shadow of the cathedral. He wished again that he had not agreed to help this girl who strode so confidently beside him.

Lara flashed him a quicksilver smile.

"Grandmother and I have friends."

CHAPTER 11

The cruck sat at the end of a twisting lane, bordered by strips of farmland. Jack had to duck his head to follow Lara into the tiny single room. There was a fire in the centre and no chimney, so that every wall – made of an earthy mix of dung, ox hair and mud – was edged with black soot. But at least it was warm. Jack wondered if the inhabitants had exercised the peasants' ancient right to fetch two cartloads of firewood from the nearby forest, though it would be rotten and crumbling.

Cramming in behind Lara, Jack saw that they would be sharing this space with two pigs and a goat, as well as the owners, Jenny and Tom.

Though Lara wore a boy's clothes and had her hair cropped close to her head, the old peasant couple welcomed her without comment, as if her appearance were nothing out of the ordinary. Jenny was soon pressing warm turnip soup and black bread pitted with grain upon them, which told of their deep affection for Lara; in order to feed their guests, neither could eat themselves.

Jack listened to Lara's chatter with something like awe as she told of her latest journeys with her grandmother to exotic places such as London and Bristol; she had even taken a sailing ship to Brittany! She spoke of the fairs they had travelled to – of strange wonders such as the carcass of an enormous lizard that could swallow men whole and a cat that was twenty times the size of a farm cat and striped orange and black.

Jenny and Tom listened with their mouths slack and the shine of wonder in their eyes.

"The only entertainment here in Wells has been the burning of Amy Middleton as a witch," Tom ventured, until Jenny put a steadying hand on his arm.

It was then Jack realised what had been bothering him about Tom. In the dimly lit room, the old peasant had been quietly tending the sleeping animals and stacking more rotten wood on the fire, without hands!

Lara heard Jack's gasp and followed his gaze. "Tom was caught trapping rabbits one winter when they were starving. They are the bishop's property and his hands were chopped off as punishment."

Sickened, Jack protested, "But Bishop Benedictus was a good man. The abbot said so!"

Lara regarded him as if he were a small child who must be told the ways of the world. "The bishop would not have known about it. His bailiff would have seen to it."

"But that is so unfair!"

Again, Lara shook her head. "There is no fairness in this world." She turned back to Jenny and Tom. "The new bishop has declared a scourge. He imprisoned Grandmother. We are rescuing her tonight and we will need your help."

Lara pulled Jack along dark streets as the cathedral bells pealed with an urgent tone. Slipping along on a slick of sewage and rubbish, they were both frustrated by and grateful for the cover of night.

Some of the people of Wells had ventured to their doors out of curiosity, but most had learned well enough to stay tucked into their cottages when the bells rang the alarm.

When Jack and Lara arrived at the edge of the moat, they could hear shouts issuing from behind the thick walls of the bishop's palace. Accompanied by the groan of protesting iron, the drawbridge was let down and a party of horsemen galloped out. The prisoners' escape had evidently been discovered!

"Over here," Lara hissed. She pulled Jack from the path of the horsemen to shelter behind a building. Then they hurried along the banks of the moat until they reached a spot roughly opposite where the prisoner had indicated that the sewer emptied into the water.

Lara gave a soft owl-like hoot and Jack marvelled at its realism. She hooted again and this time there was a soft answering splash and a dark ripple in the water.

They waited anxiously, until at last the man's head and shoulders emerged from the water, with another, frailer figure clutching tight to his neck.

Jack and Lara hauled her grandmother up the steep embankment, then strained to help the man up as well. The moat had gone some way towards washing away the unholy stink of the prison, but now both former prisoners were dripping and shivering with cold.

"Quickly," Lara urged. "Follow me!" She began to lead them on a twisting way through lanes Jack would not have suspected existed. There was no moon and they were sheltered by darkness, but the thin bars of light that escaped through tightly closed shutters still marked them out.

When a figure appeared at the end of the street, Lara hissed that everyone should stumble slightly, as if they were drunk from too much barley ale in the tavern.

"Who goes there?"

Jack froze, wishing desperately that he had the deep voice of a man. But, to his shock and relief, a strong male voice did indeed reply. "It is me, Hugh the tanner, with my sons. And who is that?" called the prisoner.

"I am Richard Pale, the bishop's man."

Jack felt his stomach cramp tightly in an agony of suspense.

"I am weary, sir, and would be thankful if you will give us leave to return home," said the prisoner.

"Very well." The man moved aside to let them pass. But, as they reached him, he shot out a long pike to bar their way. "Why are you so wet?" he demanded.

Jack bit his lip as he awaited the reply.

"It's wet work in the tannery," the big man joked. "Standing all day in a vat of piss."

The bishop's man recoiled. It was true that they

stank. But still he was not prepared to let them pass. "You said you and your sons. Who is this?" he asked in an accusing voice.

Lara clutched her grandmother protectively, trying to support her on her feet without appearing to do so.

The bishop's man used his pike to lift the edge of her grandmother's sodden hood. At the sight of the old woman's bruised and bloodied face, he drew in his breath with a sharp whistle and smiled.

Snapping into action, Jack leapt forward and pushed the man squarely in the chest. As the bishop's man struggled to regain his balance, the prisoner darted behind him and pulled him backwards, so that he lost his footing and went crashing down onto the street.

Now Jack wrested the deadly pike from the guard's slackened grip and wielded it with a rush of glory that faded the moment he realised that he might well have killed a man for the first time.

The prisoner bent over the fallen guard and felt for a pulse. "He's alive," he said. "Only knocked out."

Lara bit her lip. "He has seen us all and can report that we are four!" She tore some dirty strips from her grandmother's petticoat and rushed forward to bind the guard's arms and legs and eyes and mouth.

"Help me to hide him!"

Together, they bundled him into a cart that stood a little further down the road and Lara arranged a covering of straw over the inert body. "The peasants will get a shock tomorrow morning when they go to feed the cattle!"

It was now even more cramped in the tiny cruck. Tom and Jenny saw them in, gathered what food they could and then collapsed together on the floor, exhausted from their day's labours.

Lara sat her grandmother on the single precious stool by the fire and poured out some of the pail of well water they had used in their escape from the palace to wash the filth and crusted blood from her face. Sitting at her feet, she lovingly fed her some soup, mashing the chunks of turnip against the side of the bowl so that her grandmother would be able to swallow.

Feeling useless now that Lara had her grandmother back, Jack could do little more than watch as a transformation took place over the next few hours. Colour began to return to the old lady's ashen cheeks and her eyes, which had been dull with pain, gradually cleared as Lara pressed more herbs upon her from what seemed to Jack a magical, never-emptying pouch.

The prisoner, who had introduced himself as Nicholas, looked on with curiosity from his place next to the sleeping pigs. As Lara mixed her herbs, he queried her on the exact dosages and effects of each one.

Finally, Lara turned to him with her hands on her hips. "Why do you ask?"

Nicholas shrugged. "It is an odd skill for a kitchen boy."

"Well, what would you know?" Lara said.

"I am a doctor."

Jack and Lara turned to each other in amazement. "It was you who tended the bishop before he died?" asked Jack.

The big man nodded grimly. "I was too late. The illness had taken hold."

"What were his symptoms?" asked Lara, like one practitioner to another.

"It was the plague," said Nicholas, his eyes darting uneasily around the cruck. "Buboes, fever. You know how it goes."

Jack stiffened. Surely it was not possible . . .

"You're lying!" cried Lara. "Why are you afraid to tell us the truth? We're all fugitives now and, if

Robert Fox captures one of us, he as good as captures us all."

Nicholas sighed in apparent acknowledgment of the truth in her words. "His symptoms were cramping, vomiting, shaking fits and a terrible fever."

"Toadstool poisoning," said Lara flatly.

The man pretended to be shocked. "No, no. It was a foreign illness, caught from the Saracens. I believe it is cured with a brew of swamp frogs, chickens stung by hornets, venomous spiders, sulphur, mad dog dung, cherry pits, crocodiles stung to death by snakes and black crows drowned in salt water."

He spat into the fire in disgust. "Of course, a true doctor knows that one must roast the shells of newly laid eggs and grind them into a powder to add with chopped marigolds to warm ale."

"Why do you think they threw you in prison?" asked Lara, and Jack marvelled at her stubborn refusal to be distracted by the leech's colourful talk.

Nicholas's eyes flashed. "Robert Fox is a filthy liar. He promised me the moon and didn't so much as give me a copper. Prison was my only payment."

"And why didn't you give the bishop eyebright and milk thistle?" Lara persisted.

At this, the big man shrugged and fidgeted.

"The bishop was sick from a foreign illness," he muttered.

"Then his death is as much on your conscience as it is on that of Robert Fox," pronounced Lara. Gently, she tugged her grandmother onto a flea-bitten sheepskin and curled herself around her, turning her back to Nicholas.

Jack also tried to sleep on the earth floor. It was freezing. He thought wistfully of the abbey kitchen's blazing fire, and of blankets and wool night shoes...

Jenny and Tom were up before cock crow, dressed in the same filthy tunics they had probably worn for the entire summer. Jenny blew on the dying coals until they flared into life then added a few pieces of rotted timber.

Jack also sprang into wakefulness as Jenny settled the iron pot on the fire. He was soon up and offering to make the barley porridge. In anticipation of difficult times ahead, he had tucked a couple of cinnamon sticks, vanilla beans and ginger from the bishop's kitchen into his pouch.

Jack crumbled part of a cinnamon stick into the porridge, then threw in a whole vanilla pod, and soon the mix began to smell like something a person could actually eat. He was only sad there was no honey.

Lara and her grandmother were waking now, and Jack was relieved to see that, despite the cuts and scratches, and even a swollen purple flap of skin above one of her eyes, the herbs had done their work. The old woman's blue eyes were bright and she took her turn at eating from the pot with the single shared wooden spoon. She even managed to stand upright with Lara to assist her.

"Thank you, Jenny and Tom," the old lady said. Beneath the tremor in her voice, Jack detected flint. "We will take our leave soon. You have been very kind. For your kindness, I will tell you what I see."

Lara's grandmother turned her eyes somewhere else, as if she were searching inside. When she returned from this place, her mouth cracked into a pleased grin. "You will have children yet. The first, a boy, will arrive next winter and he will live to be an old man." At these words, Tom grunted something surly and Jenny blushed.

Jack was surprised. He had thought them old, but now, in the creeping grey light of dawn, he saw that they were simply weathered and appeared old because of constant hard work.

"Grandmother," Lara said, "there is no way of

leaving without being seen. The bishop's guards will be crawling like rats over every road from Wells."

The old lady remained calm. "Then we must travel in disguise. Tom, can you hitch the cart?"

The peasant nodded. "But it is filled with ox dung for the fields."

"Perfect," she said. "No one will search a cart full of dung."

CHAPTER 12

Jack's arms and legs ached as he lay beside Lara and the others, his bones rattling and dung flying into his mouth every time the cart trundled over a rut in the road. Tom had done a good job in covering them – too good a job.

As the cart hit another pothole, Jack suppressed a groan. Nicholas did not show the same discipline. "My stomach," he muttered from beneath the thick brown blanket of dung.

"Surely it will be soon?" whispered Lara, voicing Jack's own desperate wish.

They had heard horsemen overtake them earlier with a thud of hooves and a snorting of horses. Tom, who was leading the ox that pulled the cart, was questioned closely. In the cart, all four passengers had barely dared to draw breath beneath their layer of dung.

Tom had told his questioners that he was taking the cart to fertilise the fields and would welcome any help. He had been allowed to pass.

But at last – sweet relief – Tom halted the cart, patiently dug away the top layers of dung, and helped them out.

"Thank God," said Jack, scraping the filth from his tunic. As the others did the same, he looked about and saw that they were in a narrow ravine, with one side formed by a steep cliff and the other by a wooded slope. Except for a meandering stream and a narrow animal track, everything was covered with trees and low bushes.

"Where are we?" he asked.

Lara smiled. "You said that you would like to visit a cave. Here is your chance. We are at Wookey Hole."

They thanked Tom and helped him to reload the precious manure so that he could return and spread it across his strip of land. As the cart trundled out of sight, Nicholas paced about uneasily, looking at the cliff as if it would collapse at any moment.

Lara bustled them towards a horizontal opening in the rock partly screened by trees. "This is one of the holes," she explained, leading them deeper into a cool, damp chamber that smelled of wet earth and the coiled ferns that dripped diamonds of water at its entrance.

"We're going to stay *here*?" asked Jack, disbelieving.

"What is wrong with my house?" a gruff voice demanded from the shadows.

Lara squealed with delight. "Bertram! I didn't dare hope you would still be here!"

A bear-like man with a thick gold beard stepped forward out of the darkness, peered closely at Lara and, finally recognising her in her boy's garb, seized her up in a hearty embrace. "Then you did not count correctly." He pointed to a wall on which had been scratched hundreds of tiny vertical lines. "By my reckoning I have five more days before I may walk into Wells and declare myself a free man."

Jack realised suddenly what the man was speaking of. According to the law, if a peasant could escape from his master and live without being caught for one year and one day, he could return to the village he came from as a free man from that time on.

While Bertram embraced Lara's grandmother, Jack looked around and saw that this apparently crude cave was in fact littered with signs of human habitation. There was a small fire pit in a ledge that seemed at first to be simply a hollow. Behind a boulder, rolled up neatly, was a bed made from what looked like the roughly stitched hides of badgers and rabbits.

Two flat, disc-shaped stones lay atop each other on the ledge and Jack guessed these were for grinding grain. For a moment, Jack wondered at the idea that Bertram would risk doing something so illegal as grinding his own grain, instead of paying the lord for the privilege, then stopped to laugh at himself. As if running away was not illegal enough! He had just begun to wonder instead where Bertram got his grain from when the bear-like man asked, "And have you brought me any food?"

Lara shook her head. "Only ourselves."

"And stinking like a cesspit, too," said Bertram. "What kind of guests are these?" He pointed to what Jack had taken to be a black hole. But, as he peered closer, its surface shifted. It was an underground pool.

"In you go then," said Bertram, ushering Lara and her grandmother towards the water. "Ladies first. I still have some of your clothes here. Have a wash and we'll see what can be done."

While Lara and her grandmother bathed in what Jack imagined to be a freezing pool teeming with strange creatures, he and Nicholas followed Bertram down a set of natural rough-hewn steps into another cavern.

There, Bertram freely stoked a fire that sent flickering orange light onto the cave walls and revealed a dazzling display of giant icicles. They clung to the ceiling and rose from the floor in a strange echo of the spire-like peaks of a cathedral.

Jack breathed in the wet air with awe. "What is this place?"

Bertram straightened his shoulders, evidently proud of his abode. "This is the Witch's Kitchen," he said and pointed to one of the stalactites. "There she is – bent over her cooking pot."

Jack strained to see a witch in the massive stalactite. The fire flickered up and suddenly he glimpsed, beyond the glossy surface, the figure of a bent old woman and her cooking pot.

"She keeps me perfect company," Bertram said. "Never knew another woman who could hold her tongue and no man ever found a more perfect home. In summer and winter, the temperature does not change and there is always food in the valley, though perhaps not as much as there was in times gone by."

He rummaged behind one of the stalactites and drew out an enormous curving tusk. Stood upright, it would have come to Jack's shoulder – far too large to belong to an ox or even one of the mythical Eastern creatures with a nose for a mouth that Jack had heard spoken of.

Bertram touched the ancient tusk with satisfaction. "Now tell me how it is that you two are fortunate enough to come here in the company of Lara and her grandmother."

Nicholas seemed unwilling to speak, so Jack answered bluntly, "Bishop Benedictus has died of poisoning. And now Robert Fox has taken his place and declared a scourge."

Bertram's brow furrowed.

"He caught Lara's grandmother," Jack explained.

Now, Bertram's expression was thunderous.

"We rescued her," Jack went on, "and Nicholas is the doctor who attended the bishop's deathbed." He ignored Nicholas's pained expression as he added, "He can testify to the symptoms of poisoning."

"And you?" Bertram asked quietly.

"I am only a kitchen boy, in the service of the Abbot of Glastonbury."

"Then why are you here?"

Jack floundered. "I, ah . . . I swore to . . . er . . . Lara."

Bertram gave a knowing wink.

"It's not like that!" insisted Jack. "I felt . . ." He trailed off, unable to find the exact word. Except that it seemed suspiciously like . . . responsible. If only he had managed to lie convincingly when Robert Fox had demanded the old lady's whereabouts.

He tried again. "The scourge can be stopped. Bishop Benedictus' will –"

Bertram's warning shake of the head made Jack stop. And now the bear-like man was nodding towards Nicholas, who was listening with obvious greed. Not for the first time, Jack wondered if the doctor could be bought by the highest bidder . . .

When Lara returned from her bath, she had discarded the robes of a kitchen boy and instead wore a brightly coloured dress that gleamed in the firelight.

"Have I missed anything?" she asked.

Bertram swung about and performed a mock bow. "You look beautiful, Lady."

Jack was surprised to see that Lara did not scowl as he might have expected, but smiled with what looked like genuine pleasure.

Her grandmother had also come into the room. She stared at Jack for a moment, then finally seemed to recognise him from their encounter on the tor.

"You have a secret that you must tell the King immediately," she announced, "or all will be lost."

Jack glanced back at the narrow ravine. The cliff was lit pink with the first light of dawn and soon the cave entrance became a blue-shadowed speck behind a tangle of vines.

As Lara ducked off the track to pick a hardy, greyish-green sprig from between some rocks, Jack trudged along, thinking about the others waiting for them back in the Witch's Kitchen. He hoped that Bertram would keep a tight rein on the doctor. He did not trust Nicholas, though he fervently hoped that, if the leech *could* be bought by the highest bidder, that bidder would prove to be the King.

Now another thought occurred to him: perhaps Lara's grandmother could bring the leech to heel. Now that she was back in what she called "a place of power", her own power seemed to have magnified. During the few hours that Jack had spent in the Witch's Kitchen, it had become very obvious that it was no longer bossy Lara but her grandmother who told the others what to do. But now the thought of the old lady's calm, wizened features set doubts racing through his mind. Jack had returned repeatedly to these fears, like a tongue to the place where a tooth had been.

"And she is certain the King is in Bristol?" demanded Jack, as Lara fell into place beside him.

He had never been to Bristol, though it was only two days' ride from Glastonbury. He kicked a stone in frustration. Now that she was back in the costume of a kitchen boy, Lara's face no longer seemed pretty to him, but sharp and pinched and *knowing*. This time, he knew, there was something she hadn't thought about. It would be impossible to get from here to Bristol undetected. "The roads will not be safe."

Lara nodded. "Robert Fox's men will be swarming all over them."

"Then," fumed Jack, "how are we to get there?"

Finally, Lara seemed to register his concern. She laughed. "We will go along no road. We will walk north-west through the Mendips to the King's deer park and then you will see."

CHAPTER 13

If he had thought the cliff at Wookey Hole impressive, it was nothing compared to the great jagged cliffs they now stood upon. Lara balanced near the very edge and smiled down at the valley below, where fat black cows grazed fields stretching into the distance.

Jack tried to join Lara, but his gut revolted and his head grew dizzy as he peered down at a ribbon of silver water.

"How do we get down?" he whispered, not trusting himself to put a foot further.

"There is a goat path," Lara said. "It will take us down into Cheddar Gorge."

"This is Cheddar? Where they make the cheese?" The fine cheeses of Cheddar were often talked of in the Glastonbury Abbey buttery with competitive envy. Indeed, Jack would consider using no other when it came to a cheese and parsley tart.

Lara nodded, uninterested in such culinary matters. "There are caves in the gorge that provide as neat and dry a shelter as one could ever need." She shrugged. "Pity there is no time to stay there. Near to Cheddar is Axbridge. That is where we must go."

During their trek through the King's forest, Jack had followed Lara's confident stride, ducking fearfully behind trees at the slightest crashing of undergrowth and hardly daring to speak lest a gamekeeper discover them. Not once had he questioned her leadership. Now he said plaintively, "Why are we going to Axbridge when the King is in Bristol?"

Lara pointed down to the stream. "The river will be our road."

At another time, Jack might have been curious to visit Axbridge. He could see that this was a wool town from its heraldic symbol, carved into stone: a lamb and flag. At the crossroads they came across a bustling market, for which he and Lara could only be grateful, because the noisy crowd shielded them from the black-robed bishop's men.

They moved swiftly onwards to the rickety wooden wharves by the river, taking care to avoid those places where stallholders and townsfolk might be stopped and questioned.

Lara strode down to one of a small group of worn and leaky-looking fishing boats. It was painted blue and water-proofed with tar. A man was bent over the side, checking his woven net.

"Walter!" Lara called.

The man looked up and Jack saw a face that had been tanned red by the sun, with a hundred tiny lines crinkling around his eyes. Walter studied them – two boys dressed in food-spattered tunics – wordlessly until Lara suddenly realised what was amiss.

"It's me – Lara!"

The fisherman broke into a broad grin at this excellent joke. "I would never have known you for anything but a lad, Miss Lara."

"How are you, Walter? Are the pike biting?"

He nodded slowly. "It's been a fine season for fishing." Tilting his head in the direction of the marketplace, he added, "But it does not seem the same for the bishop's men. And you, Miss Lara. Where is your grandmother?"

A shadow passed over Lara's face and she lowered

her voice to a whisper. "We are in trouble and need your help."

Walter nodded with the same measured slowness, no doubt born of years spent bobbing on a slow-moving river, waiting for the pike to swim into his net. "Your granny saved my Annie from the plague with her caring when no churchman or leech would go near her. My life is at your service."

Lara smiled. "I don't want your life, Walter. I want your boat."

For the first time in three days, Jack actually began to relax. It was hard not to as the sun haze made him feel drowsy and the current gently pulled them closer to the sea. As the boat glided along with a rhythmic swish, Jack put his hand over the side and felt the silky water. He wondered what lay beneath those opaque green depths.

Robert Fox's men had been left behind now and they could travel without fear of detection or capture all the way down to the port of Rackley. Walter had accompanied them to ensure the safe return of his boat, and he had assured them that he had a cousin who could take them on the open sea to the port of Bristol.

Bertram had given them the leftovers from last night's meal of roasted badger, but Lara and Jack had devoured the meat early on the walk and hunger was beginning to bite once more. They were grateful when Walter shared his lunch of dark rye bread, salted fish and a wedge of cheese.

It was a scant portion, and Jack wished ardently for a sprinkling of salt, a sprig of rosemary and a lick of butter to stop the dry bread from sticking in his throat. Instead, he had to content himself with a swig from Walter's flask to wash it down and dreams of cooking fresh pike with white wine, the tops of thyme, a little mace and pepper, all of it seasoned with verjuice, salt and butter.

It was a sweet form of torture, but Jack finally gave away all thoughts of food and watched the countryside slide by in a panorama of green hills and darker green woods. Occasionally, they would pass by another boat and raise a hand in salute. At one point, Walter heaved up his nets. They had passed the boundaries of Axbridge lands and he could be fined for catching fish on another lord's stretch of river.

The world continued to glide by in a soft green and golden blur and Jack slept.

"Wake up!"

Jack woke to Lara's hands on his shoulders, shaking hard. "We've been caught in the current. You must help Walter row!"

Dazed and blinking, Jack saw that what had been a calm stretch of river he might comfortably have swum across was now a seething rush of white-capped water. They were nearing the river mouth!

Walter's face was grim as he struggled with one oar. Lara thrust the other at Jack and he seized it and plunged it into the rushing water. For the first time, he was grateful for all the lifting and carrying he had done at the Glastonbury kitchens. His arms were strong and he matched Walter stroke for stroke as they struggled to reach the shore.

"Harder!" Lara shouted. "Or we will be swept out to sea. This boat will never last."

A heaving swell of grey-brown water marked the limits of the river and it occurred to Jack that this first close-up sighting of the sea might well be his last. Dark, clumped masses of weed tilted and swayed past the lurching boat.

Jack put all his heart into matching Walter, who was rowing at the same steady pace with which he seemed to do everything else.

At last, with one final, monstrous effort, they

felt the boat slip out of the rushing current into the calmer waters of the port at the river mouth. Here, tall, steadier boats bobbed against their moorings.

Lara crowed with triumph, exhilarated by their battle with the river and the sea. She pointed to one of the tall boats and yelled to Jack over the screech of seagulls and the tearing, salt-laden wind, "It's not over yet."

Lara had behaved as though she loved every moment of the sea voyage to Bristol that Walter had fixed for them with his cousin, Seamark. But Jack had seen the greenish hue around her mouth and the way she had sneaked off to lean over the side and vomit.

In fact, it had been he who had truly enjoyed the journey, especially after spending a cramped night with Walter and his cousin and family in a flimsily constructed house that smelled of fish and rotting seaweed.

They had set off at dawn the next morning. It had been magnificent watching the sun rising over the Mendip hills to touch the sea with golden fingertips. The boat had cautiously hugged the coast, but Jack had gazed away from it to the horizon, longing to go further.

When the boat pulled into the grand port of Bristol, he had been sad to disembark. Seamark had regaled them with tales of his travels, taking wool across the channel to Wales and around to Ireland. Not for the first time, Jack wished he could adventure around the world.

Instead, Lara had dragged him into the busy port traffic, impatient to reach the King. It had been easy enough to discover where he was. Even if Bristol Castle had not dominated the harbour, the whole town was abuzz with this grand visit. The King and his court were visiting to admire the trading port of Bristol – a most valuable asset to England. And, if the King *had* intended to visit Wells while he was in the West Country, news of the bishop's death from the plague had ensured he kept his distance.

Jack and Lara hastened past a throng of men loading and unloading crates from moored vessels, and fishermen selling freshly caught fish and writhing eels straight from their boats. Only when they were in the shadow of the great castle did Lara stop. Jack watched her as she stared up at the battlements – the soaring walls looked impossible to break into.

"How will we get in to see the King? The bishop's palace was easier to get into," he asked, saying aloud what she must be thinking.

At the memory of how comparatively easily they had come and gone from the palace, the same idea struck them both at the same moment: "As the King's kitchen boys!"

Jack kept his head low as Lara marched up to the gate and demanded to be let in. The porter did not seem convinced, but finally Lara's pretended terror at the punishments they would endure at the hands of the master cook when they did not appear made him relent. After all, he could not be expected to know all of the hundreds of people who travelled in the King's retinue. And there could hardly be much danger of treachery or revolt from two kitchen boys, one skinny and the other obviously stupid.

It was easy to tell where the kitchen was. A succession of servants darted back and forth from its entrance on the right of the great hall. Jack and Lara soon lost themselves among the hundred or more souls dashing about the kitchen, stirring cream, gutting fish, breaking eggs, turning spits, powdering herbs, each working hard at their appointed task.

But, if they had planned to grab a skillet and begin the pretence of belonging, they were soon disappointed. A tall, thin man with fiery red hair approached them. "Who are you?"

Jack's eyes turned dull and he allowed his tongue

to loll a little as Lara replied swiftly, "We were told to come here by the master, sir."

"Master Gideon sent you here?" the man echoed, disbelieving.

Lara nodded. "We are skilled at sweet-making and have learned the art under a famous cook from the King's court in France." She added a few words of what might have been Oriental for all that Jack understood of it.

The man's initial disbelief now seemed tempered by something else – desperation perhaps? Or relief. "Do you know how to make marchpane, candied flowers, cheesecakes and custard flans?"

A rush of courage made Jack declare, "Better still, sir, we will create a cake that will make His Majesty praise heaven for such artistry."

The man looked surprised, but unimpressed. "You commit the sin of pride and Master Gideon will be the judge of what will grace the King's own table. But, even so, you may work over there," he said, pointing to a scratched oak bench.

Jack paced restlessly in the kitchen, listening in vain for sudden bursts of sound coming through the thick walls from the feast in the great hall. Earlier, he had seen much merriment, accompanied by a fine troupe of minstrels who played the recorder, pan pipes, zither, dulcimer and hurdy-gurdy music. Jack had been permitted to carry some of the dishes to those placed below the salt, where the lower lords and ladies sat, with their plucked brows and silver and pearl buttons on their fine silk garments.

The array of food lining the tables was dazzling. There were dishes of woodcocks, bustards, storks, gulls, mallards, curlews and cranes, as well as peacocks, larks and chickens. And that was only the fowl! Of the fish, there were more than ten varieties and the quantity of red meat upon the tables would have stocked a wealthy farm. Jack's fingers itched to take a Seville orange from a heaped pyramid that had been brought in by boat from Spain.

But the dish that concerned him most was the cake he and Lara had painstakingly fashioned from gingerbread, sugar paste and marchpane, right down to brushing on Roman numerals with a mix of saffron and gilt. It was in the shape of the moon clock, with the three ringed faces all delicately marked. The hand pointed directly up to the midnight hour and the knights and Saracens above. Further above these, Jack Blandiver waited in his tower with his bell and hammer as if to sound an alarm. On his costume, Lara had painted in elaborate, swirling red letters made from powdered sandalwood: *Jack No Name*.

The King was known to be fond of riddles and this was one that Jack desperately hoped would pay off. First, he prayed that the King would be sufficiently intrigued by the moon clock cake to look more closely in the flickering torchlight. Second, that the King would read those words and demand to know who wrote them and why . . .

The evening wore on with more muffled shouts and dancing. Lara was almost half-asleep, stirring spiced wine over the fire, when a servant burst in and raced over to exclaim, "The King praises the cake and has commanded its maker to attend him!"

Suddenly terrified, Jack looked helplessly at Lara. She shook her head. "Your name is on this one."

With sweaty palms and a dry throat, Jack wove through the tables and over the flagstones of the great hall. Surrounded by so many fine knights and ladies, he felt acutely conscious of his ragged tunic and the worn cloth leggings that bound his calves.

As he drew close to the great table, which was set up on a dais, the King gestured for the minstrels to quiet their instruments and for the acrobats to stop capering. "I expected a master cook," he said to Jack, "not a boy."

Stung, Jack replied, "I am old enough to be a squire, Your Majesty."

"A squire?" The King gave a deep, rich laugh. "Boy, your talents would be wasted polishing armour and grooming horses. Now tell me the answer to this riddle of Jack No Name, for my lords and I have spent many minutes guessing."

Jack pulled himself up to his full height. "That is my name, Sire."

The King looked disappointed. He turned to his queen and murmured something.

"But the moon clock does indeed contain a mystery, Sire," Jack ventured, his tongue dry in his mouth.

The King leaned forward. "Go on."

Jack lowered his voice. "Sire, it is a mystery that can be spoken to you alone."

Looking intrigued, the King gestured that Jack and the two noblemen who sat on either side of him and the queen should accompany him from the great hall.

Jack followed the King and his men into the solar, which was as richly appointed as the bishop's palace, with tapestries, gold vessels and elaborately carved wooden chests and stools.

"Tell me about this mystery, boy!" the King demanded.

Now that the moment had come, Jack, who had been so certain, found himself praying that he was right. But, at last, the words so long unspoken bubbled into his mouth with a rush of relief. "Sire, Bishop Benedictus' will is hidden inside the moon clock in Wells Cathedral."

CHAPTER 14

Jack could hardly believe it. He and Lara were riding into Wells with the King! Admittedly, they were tagging behind a procession of more than one hundred armoured knights, but it was thrilling to see the cheering and pointing of the people in the marketplace, and even more so to see the expressions on the faces of the market gate porters . . .

The King reined in his horse outside the cathedral and there was a great clamour and metallic clash of armour as he and his knights dismounted. Jack's heart thudded as they all proceeded through the carved porch.

Inside the cathedral, Jack was barely aware of the soaring arches and jewelled windows rising to the heavens, or of the cries of protest from the monks who were in the middle of a service. He and Lara hastened along in the company of the elderly knight to whom they had been entrusted by the King.

When they got to the northern cross-section, it was almost impossible to see ahead, for the monks had poured from the service to join the knights and now there were more than two hundred souls crammed in front of the clock.

"Jack No Name!" called the King, in a voice so deep and resonant it seemed to echo from the cavernous ceilings.

Stiffly, the elderly knight elbowed the crowd of eager onlookers out of the way and helped Jack and Lara through.

"Jack!"

Jack swung about to see Abbot Cedric reaching out a hand to stay him.

"What is the meaning of this?"

Despite the abbot's frown, Jack felt a rush of joy. Abbot Cedric looked slightly thinner for his fast but he was still alive!

"Not now, sir. I will explain everything later." If there was a later . . . for, when he reached the King, Jack saw that Robert Fox was already by his side, baring white teeth, as if he were delighted that the King should choose to surprise him with this royal visit.

Jack felt Lara squeeze his hand. A tingling

warmth passed into his palm, giving him courage, yet he trembled as they all stared up at the moon clock. The silver star pointed to the minutes: fifty-seven, then fifty-eight, then fifty-nine, then . . .

In his tower, Jack Blandiver clanged his hammer against the bell and turned his head to listen. In the same moment, the entire audience of onlookers also strained to see and hear.

Four little figures emerged from their building and chased each other in a circle – two knights and two Saracens. When the Saracen was knocked down, the King's knights gave a rallying cheer, but the deafening applause did not matter to Jack, for he had seen what he had desperately hoped he had not been imagining – a slight delay.

Now the King ordered Jack to climb up to the clock, using a knight as his ladder. There, Jack reached into the tower where the figures had retired and felt for the Saracen. He tugged it from its mount and felt inside the mechanism.

The Saracen had been cast from lead and should have been hollow. But there was something inside it now – something soft and flexible to the touch. Gently, Jack pulled out the tightly rolled parchment scroll – Bishop Benedictus' will.

The chapter house was where the priests usually met; a beautiful octagonal building on the north side of the church, lined with stone benches and a central column that soared heavenward. Jack and Lara climbed the broad, curving staircase, which seemed to flow like the rapids beyond Wookey Hole, and shared a stone bench.

This was where the King had decided to hold the trial of Robert Fox for the murder of Bishop Benedictus.

Nicholas and Lara's grandmother had been retrieved from the caves at Wookey and Bertram, too, was now legally a free man. They were to stay at the bishop's palace until the trial of Robert Fox was complete.

Jack's part in the trial was small, but he was able to testify to the near poisoning of Kitchener Payne and to say that it was he who had guessed the whereabouts of the bishop's hidden will. After that, he remained silent as he watched Robert Fox, cocksure and aggressive, claim that this was a conspiracy and that Jack and the kitchener had been put up to their parts by Abbot Cedric, who was greedy for the bishopric.

Jack was forced to restrain himself from crying out as Robert Fox accused the abbot of even worse crimes than just ambition. Anxiously, he scanned the King's face, but it showed no hint of feeling and remained impassive.

Then, as the doctor who had attended the bishop in his last days, Nicholas was called to testify. It seemed to Jack that a long look passed between the leech and Robert Fox. His fingers almost bled as he dug them into the stone bench beneath him. Would Nicholas tell the truth or be bought by the highest bid? And what *was* the highest bid? Coins? His life? If the doctor told the truth, the King might decide that he was equally responsible for the murder.

"Nicholas the Leech, what symptoms do you say Bishop Benedictus suffered on his deathbed?"

A look of oily cunning came into the doctor's eyes and Jack slumped despairingly on the stone bench. Beside him, however, Lara sat bolt upright. She seemed to concentrate her entire being on the leech so that, almost absently, he turned and caught her eye.

What he saw there, Jack could not know, but when the leech spoke, it was in a quiet, measured tone. "Sire, the symptoms were those of vomiting, cramping and raving."

"There were no buboes?"

Nicholas shook his head and replied, "The

bishop's symptoms were the same as those of toadstool poisoning."

Later, after the trial was ended and Robert Fox beheaded in the market square, Jack had his first opportunity to be alone with Abbot Cedric. While there was still doubt over whether Jack had conspired with the abbot, they had been kept in separate buildings.

Now, they walked alone in the gardens of the bishop's palace. Jack's mouth watered as he passed a flourishing patch of parsley and thought of the fine sauce he might make for . . .

"You are a good boy, Jack," said Abbot Cedric, breaking the silence.

Jack shook his head. Tears pricked at his eyes. "I swore that I would serve you and instead I left you," he said.

Abbot Cedric sighed. "If only life could be so clear, but that is the way of earthly existence. It is hard to honour an oath when a greater good beckons."

Jack looked at his feet, not knowing how to say what he must say next. "The King has asked me to go and work as his cook."

At the abbot's silence, Jack added in a rush, "I will

be able to travel with him and have many adventures and perhaps even visit the Holy Land."

The abbot nodded. "It is a very great honour."

"You don't mind then? You'll give me leave from Glastonbury Abbey?"

The abbot swept his arm out to indicate the gardens. "I will be spending more time here, now that I am also Bishop of Bath and Wells."

Jack nodded. In his will, Bishop Benedictus had stated that he wished Abbot Cedric to be his successor and the King had readily agreed with this decision.

"Besides," continued the abbot, with a twinkle in his eye, "I will still have my master cook."

"Brother Payne!" Jack could not disguise his disgust.

Abbot Cedric fixed him with his calm blue gaze. "You do not agree?"

Now that he was released from service, Jack felt free to speak plainly. "He is a drunk."

The abbot nodded. "That is why I insisted that he bring you on our journey to Wells. I couldn't stand the thought of the offal he might serve."

Jack had been watching a swan glide along the moat to tug the rope that would ring a bell for its dinner, but now he swung back to the abbot. "You knew?"

The abbot nodded. "Many years ago, Brother Payne and I went on a Crusade together. Needless to say, it was cruel and grim and I would have lost my life many times were it not for his help. But, though I was saved, something about the terrible experience, the illness and horror broke his spirit. He is a ruined man who might once have been great. It is now my turn to support him through his problems."

Jack nodded. Though he would never forget the wet rope, he began to feel some understanding, and even pity, for the unfortunate kitchener. Before he took leave to return to the King and his court, however, he had another burning question that he might only ever have one opportunity to ask. "Abbot, sir, about my parents . . ."

Abbot Cedric looked at him kindly. "You were a foundling left at the abbey gates."

"Yes," Jack pressed, "but were there any clues as to my parentage or who my mother was?"

The abbot shook his silver-tonsured head but, before he could turn his blue gaze back to the swans, Jack glimpsed something there behind his eyes. Something that made him realise that he should not dig any further, for if he did he might well find lead rather than gold.

For the last time, Jack walked with Lara through the palace gardens. Now that the scourge was ended, she was again wearing her brightly coloured dress and striding about as if she owned Wells – indeed, all of the West country and every river, rock and tree within it.

"Why did you not tell me that you knew where the will was?" Lara asked.

Jack shrugged, tired of this question. She had been plaguing him with it ever since the hurried ride back from Bristol to Wells. "I thought that, if I was wrong, you would have thought me stupid. Even more stupid, that is," he amended.

For once, Lara was neither angry nor amused. "I never thought you were stupid."

"Maybe I just felt it," Jack admitted.

Lara punched his arm. "Well, not too stupid for a kitchen knight, anyway."

Jack wondered how she knew about his secret aspirations – but then she was her grandmother's granddaughter. "Why did Robert Fox hate your grandmother?"

"He came to her for knowledge of poisoning and she would not give it. She told him only that, if he took such a dark path, he would find his doom there. He swore then that he would destroy her and all others like her."

Jack was silent as, for the first time, he truly felt how the fear of persecution lurked beneath Lara's bossy ways.

"But she is safe now," he said. "And so are the others. The abbot is a good man and will be a true bishop."

Lara nodded as she bent to pick tansy leaves from a garden bed. "Amen."

Seven years after the ordination of Abbot Cedric as Bishop of Bath and Wells, a knight and his squire rode into the pilgrimage town of Glastonbury. The knight had come to claim a manor and extensive lands bordering the abbey lands, awarded to him by the King for fine services rendered. His armour, polished to excess, shone in the late afternoon light.

They reined in outside the George Inn and a groom hurried out to take their horses. He paused to look curiously at the knight's shield, emblazoned with a coat of arms that featured a kitchen carving knife and a cabbage leaf flag.

"Make certain that our horses are well fed and stabled," the squire ordered. "Tomorrow my knight rides to Wookey to seek a fair maiden."

The groom caught the silver coin thrown to him with great enthusiasm and craned to hear the squire's last instructions, delivered in a lowered voice. "First, though, my knight requests an audience with a certain Mary Grocer, a peasant from hereabouts."

Bobbing his head, the groom asked, "Who is it that wishes to speak with her?"

The squire thrust out his boyish chest with pride. "A great favourite of the King. Sir Jack Blandiver."

This story is a fictional account set in fourteenth or fifteenth-century England. Though many details of medieval daily life are accurate, all characters and events are fictional and some licence has been taken with their attitudes, roles and setting.

GLOSSARY

almoner – monk who distributed alms, or charitable gifts, to the poor

buboes – swellings in the glands of the body

chamberlain – monk who looked after the grooming needs of the other monks

chivalry – qualities expected of a knight, such as courage, justice, good manners and kindness towards poor people

confession – admitting to a priest privately wrong deeds and bad thoughts, and asking God's forgiveness

cruck – peasant's house made of sticks and mud or clay

fast – go without food and drink

heresy – something that goes against the teachings of the church

infirmary – sick room or hospital

isinglass – substance taken from fish bladders and used to help set desserts such as jelly and blancmange

kitchener – monk in charge of the kitchen

lay brothers – men who are not monks but work at an abbey

marchpane – dessert made from almonds, rose water, sugar and eggs

medieval – belonging to a period of history that lasted for about 400 years and ended about 500 years ago

novice – young monk who has not yet taken his vows

oblate – young person who has promised to become a monk

palanquin – covered litter, or vehicle, used for carrying a passenger

portcullis – heavy iron gate

pottage – stew

Saracen – Arab or Muslim at the time of the Crusades

scourge – witch-hunting; torture and killing of women who were thought to have special powers

solar – private room for a lord

tithe – percentage of a peasant's produce that had to be given to a lord or the church

tor – hill or rocky peak

trencher – platter for serving food

vellum – fine parchment made from calfskin

verjuice – acid-tasting liquid that comes from cooking crab apples or sour grapes